Historic organ conservation

A practical introduction to processes and planning

Dominic Gwynn

Church House Publishing
Church House
Great Smith Street
London SW1P 3NZ

ISBN 0 7151 7592 0

Published 2001 for the Council
for the Care of Churches by
Church House Publishing

Copyright © The Archbishops'
Council 2001

Cover photograph by Joe Sheehan
Cover design by Visible Edge

Typeset in Sabon 11pt by
Vitaset, Paddock Wood, Kent

Printed in England by
Halstan & Co. Ltd,
Amersham, Bucks

All rights reserved. No part of this publication may be reproduced or stored or transmitted by any means or in any form, electronic or mechanical, including photocopying, recording, or any information storage and retrieval system, without written permission which should be sought from the Copyright and Contracts Administrator, The Archbishops' Council, Church House, Great Smith Street, London SW1P 3NZ.
(Tel: 020 7898 1557;
Fax: 020 7898 1449;
Email: copyright@c-of-e.org.uk).

Contents

	List of illustrations	v
	Acknowledgements	vi
chapter 1	Introduction	1
chapter 2	Organs in the Church of England	5
chapter 3	Advice and grants	15
chapter 4	Approach to organ projects: conservation versus restoration	20
chapter 5	How to cope with a restoration project	22
chapter 6	Principles of conservation	28
chapter 7	Good housekeeping	32
chapter 8	Organ building practice	41
chapter 9	Deterioration of materials	44
chapter 10	Technical matters	58
appendix 1	Grants	87
appendix 2	Advice	90
appendix 3	Bibliography	92
appendix 4	Research into historic organs	93
	Index	95

List of illustrations

fig. 1   Brightling church in Sussex: a 'west gallery' for singers, and a ca 1820 barrel organ.   7
fig. 2   Burley-on-the-Hill in Rutland.   8
fig. 3   The British mania for rebuilding.   12
fig. 4   An organ chamber with problems.   33
fig. 5   The effects of damp and inappropriate rebuilding.   35
fig. 6   Organs without roofs leave their pipes exposed to foreign bodies.   36
fig. 7   Mouse damage on the front rail of a pedalboard.   36
fig. 8   The use of inappropriate materials in the restoration of a mid-eighteenth-century windchest.   41
fig. 9   Section through an oak tree.   47
fig. 10   Corrosion of the tips of steel pallet springs.   54
fig. 11   Collapsed pipe foot.   65
figs. 12 and 13   Pipe metal corrosion.   66
fig. 14   Efflorescence of impurities from the cast metal of a reed block.   67
fig. 15   The painful results of over-zealous cleaning.   68
fig. 16   The combination of soft metal and increasingly desperate tuning.   68
fig. 17   Ciphers and runnings.   76
fig. 18   Runnings: the shrinkage of table and front rail pulls them away from the bars.   77
fig. 19   Runnings: the shrinkage of the table results in splits and failed joints.   77
fig. 20   Securing the position of loose or deformed barrel pins and staples.   85

Acknowledgements

The author is grateful to Jim Berrow, Martin Goetze and John Norman for reading and commenting on parts of the text, and particularly to the editorial work of Thomas Cocke; and also to David Knight of the Council for the Care of Churches and Sarah Roberts of Church House Publishing for their assistance in bringing the book to publication. The text is the sole responsibility of the author, who acknowledges the many faults and gaps in it, despite extensive and generous advice and assistance from friends and colleagues over the years.

With the exception of the front cover photograph, all the illustrations are from the Martin Goetze & Dominic Gwynn archive.

chapter 1
Introduction

When the Organs Advisory Committee of what was then the Central Council for the Care of Churches was founded in 1954, its agenda was markedly different from that pursued by the present Organs Committee. The press announcement, in *The Organ* of April 1954, started with the hope that the Committee 'may be the means of giving very valuable help to parishes faced with the problem of building new organs or reconstructing old ones, by putting at their disposal the advice of experts, willing to visit when necessary. Money is often wasted today on over-ambitious schemes, and also unfortunately, organ mechanisms of historic value are unwittingly discarded or spoiled by alteration.' The announcement then gave the following four 'guiding principles':

1. To oppose avoidable extravagance in organ building especially in the shape of organs larger or more mechanically complicated than is justified by circumstances.
2. To advocate the provision of the essential choruses before solo stops and other special effects.
3. To advocate the provision of adequate casework of artistic design, in a suitable position, wherever possible.
4. To oppose the re-voicing and any but minimum tonal alteration to instruments of historical importance.

There was undoubtedly concern about 'organ mechanisms of historic value' and 'tonal alterations', though what constituted alteration was less clear than it is now, and irreversible damage to historic organs continued, even by members of the Committee. More important on the agenda than the repair of old organs was the building of new ones.

The Committee recognized that organs would have to be smaller, for both economic and artistic reasons, and that temptations of maintaining the size and grandeur of earlier organs by the use of extension and electronic simulation should be resisted. If organs had to be smaller, it was time to give tonal design a decisive new direction towards the classical principles of earlier organs, and encourage a more open-minded attitude towards the historic instruments and repertoire of other European organ schools.

Another major concern was that organs should be housed in cases which were an ornament to the church and that no new organ should be without one. This concern reflected the interests of some forceful personalities in the new Committee. In the notes on church organs prepared for publication by the Council for the Care of Churches (CCC) in 1970, information and advice about cases occupied over half the space.

The success of these new directions in British organ building in the 1960s and 1970s was partial, perhaps constrained by the financial stringencies and liturgical controversies of the times, but undeniable. There is now a consensus that:

- a new organ should not be disproportionate to the church's musical needs or financial capabilities;
- its stoplist should be based around a principal chorus;
- it should be capable of interpreting a substantial amount of the mainstream repertoire;
- it should have a case with some appeal to the visual senses.

The economic pressures, in particular the decrease in funding for church music, were turned to good effect by the advisers and builders of those decades, to encourage the purchase of smaller and more attractive new organs.

On the other hand, the same period has witnessed a decline in the overall popularity of organs in churches. Fewer churches have pipe organs, or use them. If there has been a small increase in the number of new organs built each year during the last forty years, there has also been a decrease in the total stock, including some notable historic organs, lost to their particular churches and to the musical heritage of this country for ever.

In response, a new generation of advisers has set up organizations pledged to espouse the cause of friendless historic organs, encourage their retention and use, appreciate their musical value, and direct whatever funds are available towards their preservation and repair. Once again, taste and economics have moved together. While individual parishes find it more and more difficult to raise funds to spend on their music, more money has become available for historic objects deemed to be valuable to our national culture and heritage. Whatever the future for the British organ, the preservation of the most interesting examples of British organ building seems assured.

The preoccupations of the current Organs Committee reflect this new direction. Most of its business consists of assessing applications for grant aid for restoration projects, advising in disputes over the retention or rebuilding of important organs, and suggesting sources of expert advice or of alternative sources of funding. Its concern is to foster the growing respect for historic organs. For, although organs are now unlikely to be destroyed without careful consideration of their merit, valuable musical instruments still suffer from thoughtless alterations.

The available means of public funding have been increased beyond the dreams of earlier years, mainly by the addition of Lottery funding in the mid 1990s. Organs which might not have qualified for grant aid, or not sufficiently to encourage the custodians to commit themselves to a full repair, have received substantial contributions. Large projects which previously would only receive a minute proportion of the total cost in funding from public sources or the CCC can sometimes now be awarded assistance for most of the estimated cost. Overall demand for funding from the English Heritage/Heritage Lottery Fund Joint Scheme grew so rapidly in 1996/98 that a brake had to be applied to church conservation projects, including organs.

The Lottery Funds have had an effect beyond subsidy. Qualification for funding produces categories and regulations. In the case of grants from the Heritage Lottery Fund (HLF), the result has been a hearty shove in a conservation direction. A restoration project involving alterations is unlikely to be aided. With the subsidy comes advice which takes the instrument itself on its merits. The effects on builders, advisers and custodians are increasingly obvious. The Arts Lottery Fund, however, will consider grant-aiding an organ primarily as a key musical instrument enhancing a church's potential for public performances. Life will not continue as it did before the Lottery, even when the Lottery distributors change direction.

This book is a product of this changed world. It is designed to help Diocesan Organ Advisers, Diocesan Advisory Committees, Parish Church Councils and others concerned with the repair and maintenance of our stock of pipe organs to ask themselves the right questions and help them through the daunting process of reaching satisfactory answers.

chapter 2
Organs in the Church of England

What are organs for?

Most church authorities think about their organ when it starts to be a problem, either because it is becoming unreliable, or because it is ceasing to match up to the requirements of the liturgy. Some of the problems may be more imagined than real, but the questions asked will tend to be the same. They will centre around a sense of satisfaction or dissatisfaction with the organ.

Organs occupy a peculiar place in the consciousness of church people. They are large and moderately complex pieces of machinery, which require expertise to maintain and to play. Even quite small repairs can involve a congregation in projects which need a considerable effort to fund. The process of finding a competent organist is a challenge which is increasingly difficult to achieve. Since the majority of churches have only a loose allegiance to their instrument, it is not surprising that attitudes often encompass ignorance, irritation and anxiety, rather than pride and inspiration. This does not need to be the case.

On the practical side:

- organs do not have particularly complex mechanisms; certain common faults can be rectified by anyone with a rudimentary knowledge of their working; attention to their environmental stability will ensure a long and happy life;

- trained church organists may be increasingly rare, but there are still plenty of people who have learnt how to manage a keyboard; providing a little instruction and banishing a widespread fear of the extra elements which pianos and keyboards do not have would persuade more people to become church organists of a perfectly adequate standard;

- a pipe organ can be regarded as a cheap choir; one paid professional is cheaper than a choirful.

In a more positive spirit:

- the pipe organ has been the traditional liturgical instrument, capable of providing a harmonic basis to a sung unison line, and of providing ornamental music at critical points in the liturgy;
- its effect on the listener is a matter of taste and custom, but when instrument, player and music are in sympathy the result can inspire awe and reverence;
- a pipe organ, as a work of craftsmanship, and as a vehicle for a musician, is an expression of ideas at the centre of our civilization's appreciation of aesthetics.

After these ringing endorsements for the pipe organ, it may be disappointing to return to the experiences of many churches with their organs. In most, it has a job of work to do: setting the atmosphere before a service, accompanying hymns, filling embarrassing silences, making a noise at moments of joy and praise. It may seem as if those commissioning and building the organ had no higher ambition than to provide a machine with the sounds appropriate for these tasks but there is much more to be derived from the great variety of experiences, reflected in the long history and diverse musical traditions of the Church of England.

A brief history

Only a handful of church organs survive from before the Civil War. The organs installed in the early part of the seventeenth century as part of the so-called Laudian emphasis on well-conducted liturgy were generally confined to the Chapels Royal, college chapels in Oxford and Cambridge and cathedrals. The first major increase in the provision of organs elsewhere was in the city of London after the Restoration of 1660, emulated in the eighteenth century by major parish churches in the provinces. It was made possible by increasing commercial prosperity channelled through charitable giving and the church rates, and prompted by a desire for seemliness and order in church services.

Organs in the Church of England

By 1800 most of the parish churches in the major provincial towns had an organ, along with a Sunday school choir, to control and augment the congregational singing of the psalmody.

In the 1830s and 1840s there was a struggle within the Church, which tended to be accompanied amongst the reforming tendency by a desire for beauty and elaboration in the fabric, furnishings and liturgy of the Church. Over the following three or four decades, organs became an essential part of a church's fittings, high on the list of a reforming vicar's priorities, after the replacement of box pews with open pews or chairs, and the provision of a stove. In 1840 only the parish church of the main town would have had an organ, and perhaps the parish church of a large aristocratic estate. By 1880, almost every church would have had an organ accompaniment of some sort, ousting the singers, the band and their gallery. Whereas organs provided before 1840 tended to be placed on a west gallery, after 1840 there was an increasing migration towards the floor and, if at all possible, to the chancel, where the organ was in close proximity to clergy and choir.

Some of the organs provided would have been rather shoddy or inexpertly made, but by 1914 almost every church would have

fig. 1 Brightling church in Sussex: a 'west gallery' for singers, and a ca 1820 barrel organ, with a monument to the squire who gave the gallery, the instruments to accompany the singing, and the organ.

Historic organ conservation

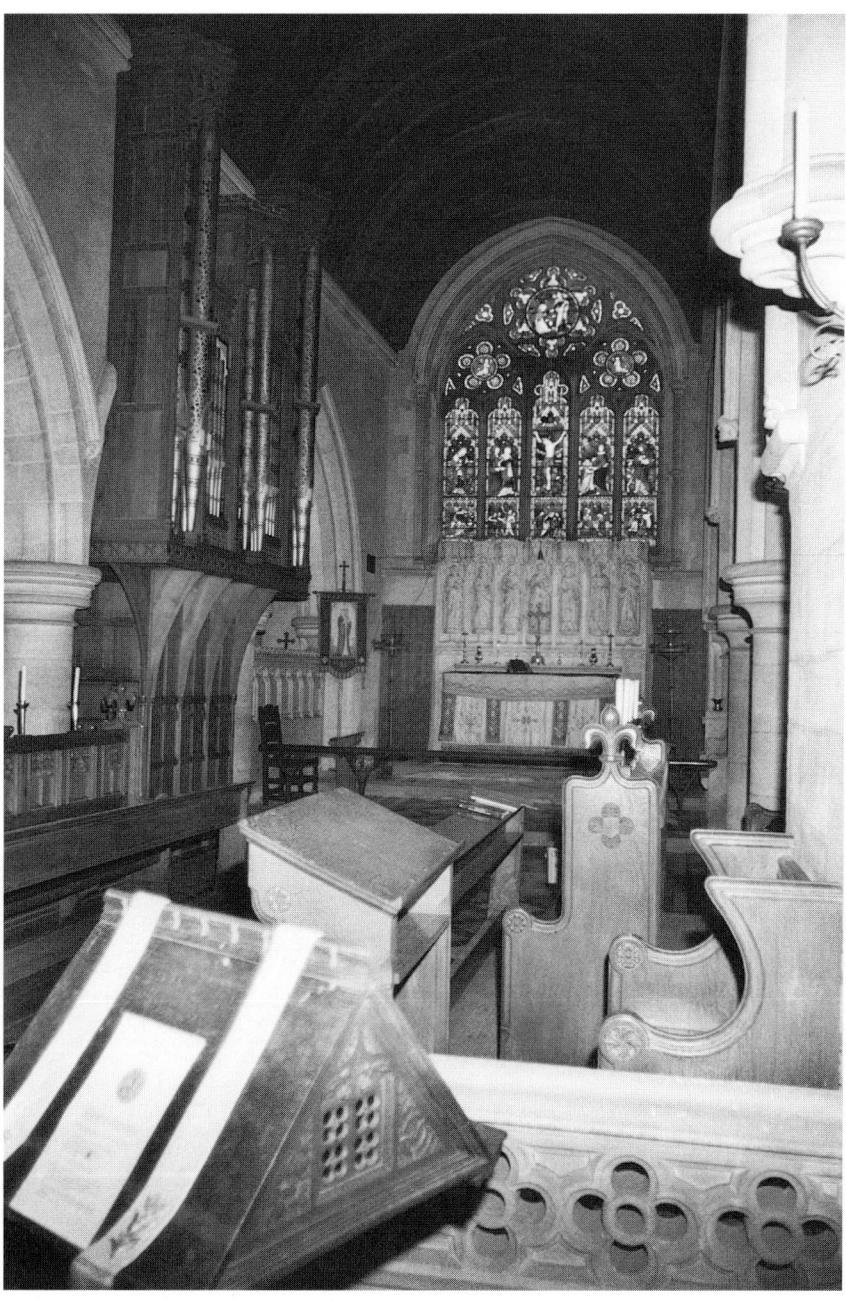

fig. 2
Burley-on-the-Hill in Rutland: an ecclesiologically correct chancel, with choir pews and chancel organ.

had an organ of a more or less standard type, played to a fair degree of competence, either by a trained organist, or by the spouse of the vicar, squire or one of the local professional men. It would have supported congregational hymn-singing from a hymn book which was one of the fruits of the mid-Victorian reforms in the liturgy, encouraged elements of a choral service, or accompanied ambitious choral works performed by large and enthusiastic choirs. Around 1914 too, there began a way of improvising on the organ which was devised to encourage feelings of piety and reverence. Cecil Clutton wrote in 1976 that it was Sir Hugh Allen at New College in the 1920s who first made an organ 'smoke', which serves to remind us that the Victorian organ was not primarily designed to provide atmospheric music.

Not all organs were new; many were comprehensively rebuilt. The more important churches tended to exchange their organs for bigger and more up-to-date versions, and smaller and poorer churches took their leavings. Only rarely did an out-of-the-way church manage to subsist on an instrument from the old dispensation, or without an organ at all.

The situation in 1914 can be said to represent the high point of British organ building; from that point it slowly declined. The desire for large numbers of stops of differentiated tone colour did not lessen, but the money to supply it did. Instead of new organs, or radical rebuilding, organs tended to be re-arranged and tinkered with: bits were added, means were devised to get more out of fewer pipes and, finally, standards of craftsmanship started to fall.

This situation did not change immediately after 1945, but very gradually the perspective on what constituted an organ altered. In a few places, new organs were built which were based on the structure of the principal chorus, and, from the end of the 1960s, with mechanical key action. The aim was to inject into a moribund craft a new energy, and a fresh immediacy for player and listener. The impetus was provided by the Organ Reform Movement in Northern Europe, where such organs had become orthodox, but for lack of money and an insular suspicion of continental developments, the movement in England remained very small.

It was enough to inspire a small group of future players, advisers and builders, however, and their experiences and determination to change the course of British organ building have resulted in a new orthodoxy, not, in the end, a Bach organ, but an organ from the English classical tradition, as it had developed during the high Victorian period.

The result is an increasing unity of purpose amongst advisers and builders as to what sort of organ should ideally be provided and as to how older instruments should be retained and repaired. There are still threats to the pipe organ, from a lack of money, electronic alternatives, and popular forms of music making, but there is a sense that the organ building industry has recovered its standards after a perceived low point in the 1970s.

The surviving organs

Organs in England must be the most frequently altered of any in Western Europe. Relatively few survive intact from the classical period. Most churches have an organ built or rebuilt in the period from around 1880 to 1914. These were organs of pronounced character, which have seemed increasingly unpalatable more recently, as liturgical practice and musical taste have changed. The history of the organ at St Lawrence Whitchurch at Edgware in Middlesex is typical of this development, although the Baroque decoration of the interior is far from standard.

built	1716	one manual	seven stops
rebuilt	1848	two manuals and pedals	twelve stops
	1877	two manuals and pedals	fifteen stops
	1913	two manuals and pedals	sixteen stops
	1949	two manuals and pedals	thirty-two stops
new organ	1994	two manuals and pedals	fourteen stops

A gradual increase in size is obvious. There were also changes in the stoplist which meant that by 1949 the only 1716 pipes remaining in 'Handel's organ' were the front pipes and 44 pipes in the Swell Open. Needless to say, there was a great deal of extension in the 1949 organ. The mechanism was completely replaced in 1877, much of it again in 1913, and again in 1949. Apart from the few surviving remains from 1716, the whole organ was replaced in 1994, using the 1716 parts as the inspiration.

For a large town church, the history of the organ at St Mary's, Nottingham, is equally instructive (information abstracted from Abbott and Whittle, *The Organs and Organists of St Mary's Church Nottingham*, 1993):

built	1705	one manual	
rebuilt	1742	two manuals	thirteen stops
new organ	1777	three manuals and pedals	twenty-two stops
rebuilt	1838	three manuals and pedals	twenty-three stops
rebuilt	1867	two manuals and pedals	twenty-two stops
new organ	1871	three manuals and pedals	thirty-eight stops
rebuilt	1902	three manuals and pedals	forty-one stops
new organ	1916	three manuals and pedals	forty-two stops
new organ	1973	two manuals and pedals	twenty-five stops

It is unusual even for an important church to have no fewer than four new organs in the last three hundred years. The last instrument is a modern neo-classical organ, not a reconstruction around the surviving parts of the 1777 organ, although that is still possible, for they were moved to another church. Perhaps there is still room for further developments at St Mary's.

The history of the organs in these two churches has not quite turned full circle, but the pattern is clear. The original organ was quite small, with a lively and clear tone. As the organs became larger, with more stops of differentiated character, the tone became duller and more opaque. The latest step has been to return to the smaller but more energetic organ.

The Nottingham example also shows some typical features in siting the organ. The earliest organs stood on a screen between nave and chancel. The 1777 organ was placed in the west gallery, which accommodated an important amount of the required seating, and a space for the children's choir which assisted the

Historic organ conservation

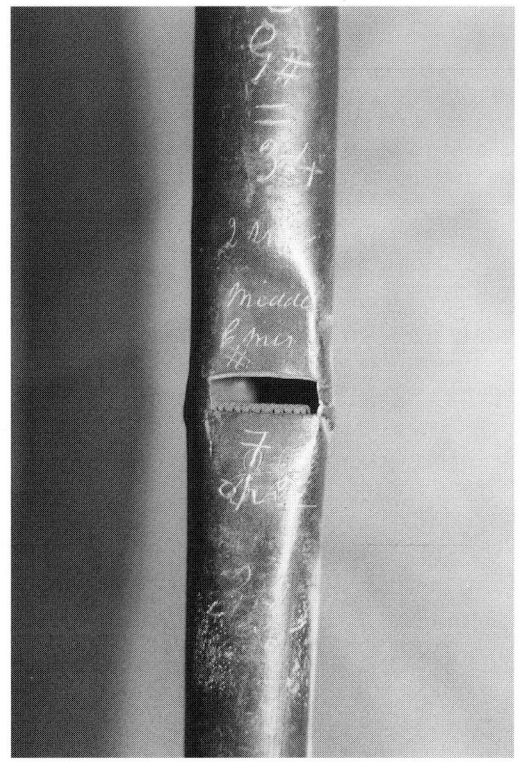

fig. 3
The British mania for rebuilding: this pipe has stood in four different positions in its life.

psalmody. The 1871 organ was moved to the east end, as part of a large re-ordering and restoration programme. Unfortunately there was not really enough space in the chancel, and the organ suffered from damp against the north wall. It was replaced by an organ which stood in the south transept, where it was cooked by the new heating plant. The 1973 organ is hung on the east wall of the south transept, a position which seems characteristic of the modern dilemma about organ siting, reluctant as we are to replace the galleries on which organs generally stood until the mid nineteenth century.

Problems and dilemmas

These are unusual examples, but many organs have suffered a similar history of alteration. On the whole, the stronger the musical tradition the church has, the more likely its organ is to be altered. The result is that the English classical organ has all but disappeared, and even the Victorian organ has suffered almost wholesale removal of some of its features, as Nicholas Thistlethwaite discovered when writing his book *The Making of the Victorian Organ*.

Alterations do not necessarily spoil an instrument. Some important historic organs, both in England and overseas, are the products of two or three different periods, for instance with late-eighteenth-century Great and Choir organs, and a High Victorian Swell and Pedal.

These alterations can be insidious, a constant drip feed of money and a constant feeling of dissatisfaction with the organ causing endless tinkering: transposition of ranks of pipes from one stop to another, re-voicing or 're-balancing' of individual ranks, re-naming stops, electrification of parts of the action, spraying gilded front pipes with gold paint, removing ivory keys and replacing them with plastic, repositioning the organ in the church, etc. There comes a point when the original organ hardly exists any more.

Restoration is almost always feasible. It may be that tonal alterations have taken the organ a long way from the original. It may be that environmental damage has left the organ with serious problems. But it is nearly always possible to restore altered or deteriorating organ parts to working condition.

The desire to restore

An organ may seem dull or inadequate as a musical instrument, but it should always be remembered that it was bought for a purpose, and that it satisfied a previous generation. It may be that with a little care and affection, and with the right attitude, even the least prepossessing organ can help to raise the voices of the people and with some appropriate music bend their thoughts to holy things.

A pipe organ is an asset which either depreciates slowly or increases in value. Do not get rid of it unless absolutely certain that future generations will thank you for it. Too many PCCs regret the actions of their predecessors.

It should never be forgotten when estimating costs that the organ, even if it is the most significant piece of hardware, is only one element in a church's musical life. The cost of purchase and upkeep should be part of a budget that includes the organist's salary, purchase of music, choir expenses, other instruments and accessories.

chapter 3
Advice and grants

Statutory bodies

In other countries in Western Europe, they do things differently. In some countries organs, like the churches they stand in, belong to the state; historic organs are protected by statute, and are in the custody of a government department. In others, a similar system is exercised by the churches, but because it is funded from a church tax, handed down from top to bottom, the effects are rather similar. Policy is formulated at a central point, and is interpreted and administered by a small handful of advisers. The congregation is required to contribute very little money towards the work, and usually has correspondingly little influence on the outcome. This kind of system, like all benevolent despotism, appears ideal but can have disastrous consequences.

The Anglo-Saxon way is more pluralistic. The nearest we come to a statutory body is English Heritage (EH), but they have proved reluctant to become involved in organs as working instruments, confining their grant-giving to organ cases. The situation has become blurred in recent years through EH's role as chief adviser to HLF, which does finance the restoration of historic instruments.

The statutory controls on buildings and their fittings do not include organs, even when they are owned by public bodies. Organs are only protected when they enter the possession of museums or of institutions such as the National Trust. In churches, organs, like other fixtures and furnishings, are protected by the faculty jurisdiction. This should concern itself with all alterations, visible, mechanical and tonal.

Grant-giving bodies

As was mentioned before, funds have been made available for organs from the proceeds of the National Lottery for the arts and for the heritage. It should, however, be remembered that the criteria of the funds are not necessarily those of Church of England parishes. If the application is for a new organ, there is usually a requirement to make the organ available to the wider community. If it is for a restoration project, the significance of the instrument and the importance of the project are seen in terms of cultural heritage, not in those of parish worship.

If aid for a new organ is sought, the Lottery Fund concerned is administered by the Arts Council. The most useful sources of information and advice with the preparation of applications are the Regional Arts Boards and the national Arts Councils. For restoration projects, application should currently be made through the Joint Grant Scheme for Churches and Other Places of Worship, administered jointly by EH and HLF. Arrangements may alter after the Joint Scheme is reviewed in 2001.

The sums which were available before the Lottery still exist and are as important as ever, not only for the relatively small number of parishes which will not use the Lottery funds, but to obtain partnership funding and to fill the gaps where the criteria of the Lottery funds do not apply. Through its Organs Committee, the Council for the Care of Churches administers the funds made available by a number of charitable trusts, notably the Pilgrim Trust and the Esmée Fairbairn Charitable Trust. These modest but useful grants often come with advice, and back up the criteria underpinning the faculty system.

There are several charities which may give assistance for organ restoration schemes, though their contributions are sometimes limited to particular geographical areas or periods. The sums available are not large and applications have to be handled by each body in its own way, at its own time and according to strict criteria. All the same, they can provide a significant boost to the fundraising effort.

Applications to grant-givers can be daunting affairs in terms of time spent collecting the relevant information and presenting the case. For smaller grants, the work is correspondingly less, but searching for likely funds, ploughing through the directories and following the leads still require stamina.

Raising the money is a crucial part of the problems involved with restoration projects, but it is only a part. Identifying the correct

Advice and grants

course of action can also be intimidating. A significant development in the organ world in the last two or three years has been the establishment of formal organizations for advisers and builders, following the lead given by the Lottery Funds in setting down the criteria for advice.

Voluntary bodies

For organs in parish churches, control and advice are provided in the first place through the Diocesan Advisory Committee (DAC) and its Diocesan Organ Adviser (DOA), supported by the Organs Committee of the CCC; the first approach should always be made to the DOA.

The position of the DOA is to advise the DAC, who in turn advises the Chancellor on the granting of a faculty, though in practice he or she often provides free advice to the church as well. It may be that the DOA has the time and the experience to become more closely involved with a restoration project, but it is also possible to engage a consultant with specialist knowledge. There is now a body that puts owners in touch with a suitable adviser, the Association of Independent Organ Advisers (AIOA).

Usually a consultant or a DOA will advise on suitable organ builders, but there may be circumstances where a church wishes to pursue its own project, or wishes to check on the advice being given. The Institute of British Organ Building (IBO) was set up in 1996 as a professional association for the organ building trade. Its members are described in a register, available from the Secretary. It is increasingly likely that grants will only be awarded to projects using a builder accredited for historic restoration.

The British Institute of Organ Studies (BIOS) seeks to influence the fate of historic organs by offering education and information. Education is provided through its publications, which make current research available, and through its conferences, which reveal the character of historic organs and the music written for them. BIOS has also alerted custodians of historic organs to their importance, particularly if the network of enthusiasts has revealed unwise proposals. It is trying to pre-empt misguided actions by

chapter 4
Approach to organ projects: conservation versus restoration

There are always good reasons for restoring a pipe organ, and also good reasons for restoring the organ to its original condition, or for leaving it at some viable point in its building history rather than adding to it. A musical instrument which has a definable character will always attract more pride and interest than an organ which is a mongrel.

Arguments for restoration

- In the same way that the value of an art object is reduced if it is altered, an organ will be of less interest and less valuable if tampered with.
- An organ which has been altered is often more difficult to maintain, and can be more difficult to play.
- The next generation often regrets the actions of the previous ones; the work of each generation has more value as it gets older, and the less it is altered.
- Regular maintenance and a suitable environment for an existing instrument will save money in the long term; there is no point spending money on new work if that will be damaged by adverse conditions within the building.

Approach to organ restoration

An organ in its original condition, without apparent or hidden alteration, is rare in this country. Most restoration projects face the problem of coping with a rebuilt, and sometimes a much rebuilt, organ. The answers to that problem are rarely straightforward. It is increasingly acknowledged that the requirements of current musical and liturgical fashions are not sufficient reasons in themselves for alterations.

The following questions need to be asked:

- How much of the original material remains; does it justify a return to the original state? Does enough survive or is there sufficient evidence to make a convincing reconstruction of the original?
- If the organ is restored to an earlier state, would any significant work be lost? Would it be more conservative and less intrusive to return to a later rebuild, which was the coherent expression of the last artistic ideal?
- What was required for its original use, and what is required for its anticipated use? Can the two be reconciled? Is the organ so disturbed by repeated rebuilds that only a rationalization process can make sense of it?
- Can the organ teach us anything about our traditions? If restored to its original state, will its potential in one area compensate for loss in another?
- Are the desired alterations a question of comfort for the player or necessity?

It helps to be pragmatic. An organ may be so limited by the constraints of its period that it can perform few of the functions required today and so will not be used. The use of a seventeenth-century tuning system, or of an eighteenth-century short-compass swell, are not often within the competence of today's organists. Opinions will, however, vary. The restoration of a Victorian swell organ may seem eminently useful to one person, the preservation of the organ as found may seem sensible to another. There is never one answer, even within the generally conservative principles set out in this book.

The conservative route is winning more and more friends. The rewards of playing historic organs become more appealing. Builders rediscover the joys of working with old materials and techniques. The duties of preserving the heritage become more apparent. And most persuasively of all, the amount of money available for preserving is increasing.

chapter 5
How to cope with a restoration project

Advice and advisers

The first step is always to get in touch with the Diocesan Organ Adviser (DOA), who can be contacted via the DAC Secretary or the Archdeacon. The primary job for DOAs is to advise the Diocesan Advisory Committee about all organ matters, but they are often well qualified to give general advice to parishes on their instruments. If it is a question of applying for a faculty, the process is likely to run more smoothly if the DOA has been kept informed throughout. A parish may also decide to appoint a consultant in more complex cases, because he or she has special knowledge of that particular organ or that type of organ. If so, he/she will usually be paid, at least expenses, but usually also a fee which may be a proportion of the cost of the project, an hourly rate or an agreed sum.

An adviser/consultant has a role to play both in restoration projects and in new work, especially where options are not clear-cut. The general knowledge and experience of the adviser can guide the specialist knowledge of the builder. Advisers ought to be able to draw up an inventory of the parts, recognizing date and provenance, and set out the principles which the restoration will follow, detailing which parts will be retained and which repaired, removed or replaced. They should be able to provide answers to problems, for instance in finding suitable models from which to replace missing parts, monitor progress and, finally, to check and approve the finished work. The DOA may be able to advise on a consultant but the AIOA or the Organs Committee of the CCC can also put churches in touch with the appropriate advisers. BIOS can provide a report and advice where the organ is of obvious historical importance.

Preliminary survey

Before embarking on any significant work, it is important to compile a survey of the organ. The survey should cover three areas:

- the history of the instrument's development, from the original builder through subsequent rebuilds and restorations, to the present;
- the inventory of the organ, attributing and dating the parts, and assessing the alterations made during the rebuilds;
- an assessment of the current condition, describing faults and suggesting the nature and scope of the restoration work.

It is not necessarily the consultant who should make the survey. Another expert, perhaps an organ builder, might be asked to take it on, particularly if they happen to have specialist knowledge of the work of the original builder. The survey will form a major part of the brief to which the estimating builders will work, though it may be altered in the light of later examination, particularly while the organ is being dismantled. The parish, having studied the survey, must decide what it wants to do and circulate a reasonably detailed brief. It is also essential to have prepared the survey before approaching grant-giving bodies. It is wise to make the first approaches at this stage, though most grants will only be confirmed once the builder has been chosen. Some trusts only want one approach, with a concrete proposal, including the chosen builder's estimate, but for larger grants it is advisable to approach the grant-maker before estimates are sought.

Raising money

The determination to raise the necessary funds is an essential part of any organ project. It requires tenacity to apply for grants and to raise money locally but it is worthwhile exploring every avenue. The allocations of the major funds may not apply to the case whereas awards by more local and smaller trusts can raise awareness in the district. Local fundraising, even if it raises a comparatively small amount, has the inestimable value of binding the local community to the project, as well as providing the matching funding which most trust funds require.

Part of the work required in applying for grants consists of discovering the different requirements of different trust funds. It should also be noted that the landscape of grant-giving changes frequently. The DOA and/or the consultant to the scheme should have expertise as to the way current grant-giving works. Information on relevant trusts and charities is given in appendix one.

Estimates

Estimates should always be required. If the project costs less than £5,000, there is no need to ask for more than one; if it costs more, it is advisable to have three.

The brief should be as precise and complete as possible (see above) and should ask each builder to provide a quotation for similar work, so that direct comparisons can be made. Builders' estimates should be fairly detailed, giving the cost of each part of the work. The conditions should be set out clearly.

Beware of estimates that allow the cost to be raised in the final invoice. It is better to receive a binding estimate at the first inspection, which can then be renegotiated later if problems turn up. Experienced restorers will recognize danger signs and should be able to make their original estimates conditional on their suspicions. The important thing is for parish and builder to develop a relationship of trust and to keep in touch constantly. The feeling that the customer is keeping a close eye on events is an added incentive to a builder to keep up standards.

Value Added Tax

The interpretation of the legislation has in the past varied somewhat from one VAT office to another, but since the issue on 27 September 1997 of the *Guidelines for VAT on Church Organs* rules have been standardized. Any work on existing organs that can be classed as repair or maintenance is standard-rated. Work on old or historic organs can only be zero-rated if it is made as part of a scheme of 'approved alterations' to a listed building. The alterations must be to the structure or the fabric (roof, walls, floor, etc.), and must not involve repair or maintenance. The organ does not count as fabric in itself. Where the work does involve 'approved' alterations to the fabric, then whatever is done to the organ is zero-rated, including replacement of an existing organ with another old organ.

The choice of organ builder

It is advisable to approach a builder who has an established reputation in the organ world. A builder who is already caring for the organ should be considered but a tuner is often not capable of complicated restoration work. Occasionally a team of enthusiasts has carried out effective repair work which has stood the test of time, but for every successful project of this sort there have been a hundred which range from regrettable to disastrous.

When choosing from whom to obtain estimates, it is advisable to choose different kinds of firms, with different qualities:

- A large firm may be based some way off, it may be expensive and the person you deal with may not be the person who is doing the work, but it has resources and experience which will include a large tuning round and it may have all-round expertise.
- A local firm is likely to identify more closely with the project but might not have the experience or the resources to cope with the whole project. It should also be better at dealing with on-going maintenance.
- It may also be worth considering a firm that has a particular knowledge of a particular organ type or which has acquired a reputation for skill in the restoration of historic organs.

It is essential for the parish or its advisers to ask for references from previous customers, to visit the workshop and also examine previous work, to ascertain the standard of craftsmanship and the efficiency and personality of the builder.

Faculty permission

Unless the work involves no more than running repairs, permission will be required which is granted in the form of a faculty. For most organ work which involves 'repairs using matching materials', the faculty will be granted by the archdeacon, following consideration by the DAC. For more complex projects and new organs, or where the DAC declines to recommend a scheme, the matter is considered by the Diocesan Chancellor. The process is now strictly enforced and contravening it can lead to expensive consequences.

The cooperation of the DOA is highly desirable to ensure that the application runs smoothly but, if the church feels strongly in favour of a proposal, it can apply for a faculty despite a negative recommendation from the DAC.

Contracts

Once an organ builder has been chosen for the project, the terms of the contract and method of working should be negotiated. Something of the builder's usual practice should already be known, since it bears on their suitability for the job, but further details will need to be established before the contract is signed.

Generally speaking, two things should be watched with care: open-endedness in the contracts and hidden costs. While it has to be accepted that major restoration work can rarely be predicted with certainty, some controls need to be set on expenditure.

Some conservators insist on working on a time and expenses basis, although customers may find that they cannot be certain how much will be spent by the end of the project. Others revise the amount in the final instalment to take account of unscheduled extra work or under-estimated costs (sometimes under the cloak of inflation). Most work to a fixed price which, if they are sensible, is towards the upper end of the probable cost. A fixed price is essential for certain grant applications, and for fundraising appeals. The happy mean is to try and establish a reasonable fixed cost with some degree of flexibility and to keep both builder and client informed at all stages of the work.

There are always unexpected costs. These usually arise in those areas of the work which are directly under the control of the church: e.g. electrical work in the church, scaffolding, and board and lodging for the builders during the work. The church may feel it can save money in certain areas without jeopardizing the standards of the work, but they should always be budgeted for before the project starts. There are charges relating to financing of projects, like VAT, insurance and bank interest charges which cannot be avoided and need to be established clearly at the beginning. Finally, there are extras which a reputable and experienced restorer is most unlikely to impose; make sure who is paying sub-contractors and that everyone fully understands exactly what is to be done for the money.

Payment

The instalment system of payments is usual, but arrangements vary from builder to builder. Make sure you understand what is involved. To pay too early can lead to expense in obtaining bank finance. Alternatively, not to pay up until the final assessment does concentrate the builder's mind. It is important to pay the invoices as they arrive. It is a fortunate organ builder whose cash flow is so healthy that it can withstand constant late payment.

Guarantees

It is not always possible to give a guarantee for partial repairs, but if a comprehensive restoration is undertaken, a guarantee should certainly be provided. It is difficult when working on an old organ to show that faults are the result of the builder's inefficiency rather than the organ's unpredictability, but a guarantee of ten years, for instance, does help to underline the restorer's responsibilities.

chapter 6
Principles of conservation

Ideally, all work on organs should be carried out according to the following principles, which are based on those of the International Institute of Conservation:

1. All work should be researched beforehand, to enable the correct decisions to be made. No work of restoration should be undertaken if the environment is unfavourable; apart from the waste of money, the organ will suffer if it is subject to constant repairs caused by damp, dry or corrosive atmosphere.

2. The character of the organ should be respected; adding to or altering parts of the organ in a way alien to its tonal or visual character is irresponsible, both for the instrument itself and for those future generations who may want it to speak in its authentic voice.

3. Any work should be capable of being undone, even after time, so that the organ can be returned to its pre-restoration condition; our generation is not omniscient, nor is our taste likely to remain unquestioned.

4. As far as possible, the decayed parts should be repaired rather than replaced; a restorer should always try to retain and repair original parts, from action buttons to tuning systems. The consequences of ageing should not be disguised or removed; part of the charm of old things is that they are old and testify to the continuity of church life.

5. All work should be adequately documented, for the benefit of future owners, restorers and researchers. Copies of the restoration report should be deposited in the church log book, the organ builder's records and, in significant cases, with the CCC.

Principles of conservation

These principles can be summarized as:
1. adequate preparation;
2. respect for the character of the organ;
3. reversibility of restoration techniques;
4. minimum intervention;
5. full record of restoration work.

All organs, whether ancient or modern, should be looked after similarly if they are to remain in a condition for which our successors will thank us. Quite apart from musical issues, financial prudence indicates that the more care expended in the short term, the less will be required in the long term.

Terms and definitions

A glossary of restoration terms, agreed by everybody, is probably impossible. For some, the term restoration implies a rebuild; for others, conservation is a dirty word. Nevertheless, here is a contribution towards bringing some useful meaning to the key words.

Conservation: preservation of the existing materials in the condition in which they are found, a course which cannot always be followed if an organ is to be brought back to working condition.

Rebuilding is usually held to involve obvious alterations or additions to the existing organ in a different style. Any alteration which can be seen from the keys would be considered 'obvious', that is, changes in the stoplist, key compass, etc. If a rebuild is so radical that the result is virtually a new organ using older parts, it is sometimes sold as a new organ, a definition which builders of organs with newly manufactured parts would understandably dispute.

Renovation is a more emotive term but it neatly describes the kind of wholesale replacement of parts which constitutes much 'restoration'. 'As new' may be acceptable when applied to the way the restored parts work, but not when applied to the way they look.

Repair: the word most used and most generally understood. Whatever the method used, any worn or damaged part that is healed, put into splints or given crutches can be said to have been repaired.

Restoration: returning the organ to some point in its history, a revival of the original or previous state. However, attempts at restoration usually involve some compromise. The word is usually interpreted as, at best, 'bringing back to playing condition', at worst, 'preserving the character of the original', which can mean that the substance is largely discarded. Where the restoration is far-reaching, i.e. only half the original organ survives but that is chosen as the model for the project, it might be more honest to use the word 'reconstruction'.

The indistinctness in the boundaries between definitions is obvious, but this reflects how their changes in meaning follow evolving attitudes. The word 'restoration' would not have been used in its current sense fifty years ago, when it would have been foreign to all thinking in the organ world at the time.

The problem is compounded by the fact that many projects combine a mixture of approaches. Since it is so rare to find a historic organ in completely original condition, the competing requirements may result in a compromise which involves conservation and repair of the surviving original parts, reconstruction of missing parts and additions which are nothing to do with the organ's history. The crucial goal is for those involved in a restoration scheme to be prepared to give the instrument priority over musical fashions and workshop practice.

The rights of the organ

A revealing alternative way of examining attitudes towards a historic organ can be expressed through the following contrasts:

restore the organ to its original condition	destroy its building history
restore it to a point in its building history	reverse its building history
repair it as found	freeze its building history
bring it into line with modern thinking	continue its building history

These pairs of interpretations of the same processes show how apparently simple statements can become quite complicated. Just using the words 'rebuild', 'restoration', 'repair', 'conservation', either correctly or incorrectly, produces unexpected reactions and results.

The questions 'Is this organ historic?' and 'What should we do with it?' receive different answers, depending on the individuals involved, whether the owner or custodian, the clergyman, church council, organist or congregation, regulating bodies, the voluntary monitoring associations or the CCC. The organ itself cannot speak in words but it is nevertheless eloquent witness through its music to our heritage of past repertoires and past ways in which the liturgy was accompanied.

This witness becomes more significant as the evidence disappears. Concern about alteration and decay becomes greater as the organ's character becomes fugitive. Our desire to hear the music as it was originally performed increases as the means diminish.

If economics, tradition and culture can be made to combine, something will be achieved. In a prescient pamphlet, *On the Care of an Organ*, Andrew Freeman encouraged parishes to look after their organs; 'money spent now will prove less costly in the end than neglect'. Good housekeeping and a lightness of touch in keeping the organ going will ensure a longer life and lower expenditure.

chapter 7
Good housekeeping

Introduction

Churches have similar environmental problems to other buildings. A congregation should aim to make the environment as stable as possible and to keep alert to potential problems before they require expensive repairs. The care with which an organ is treated as an instrument or as a piece of furniture will help to prolong its life.

A record should be kept of faults and short-term repairs. There should also be a formal arrangement with the builder to look after the instrument, even if visits are only on an annual basis.

The organist should listen for the effects of dehydration; it can cause damage which requires drastic repair work. It is heralded by runnings (wind sounding other notes than the ones intended), easy stop movement, changes in the key depth and wooden stopped pipes suddenly going sharp or losing their speech. Sounds of wind leaking may be mechanical, but may also be caused by leather hardening or cracking, or being eaten by mice, joints coming apart or even pipes leaving their holes for some reason. Woodworm holes should be watched for new dust, especially in early summer.

Attention should be paid to the surroundings of the organ, as if it were a piece of furniture of one's own. Care should be taken that there is not too much traffic around the organ, that there is no heater or light too close, that damp or crumbling patches of wall next to the organ are dealt with, that neighbouring windows are weather-proof and that outside drainage is adequate. Rainwater goods should be checked regularly, and any faults in the roof quickly dealt with. As to the cases, antique pieces of furniture do not like drawing pins, light fittings, screws, hooks or any of the other insidious pieces of vandalism perpetrated by otherwise sensible people.

Good housekeeping

Security is always a difficult matter for churches, and it is impossible to be completely vandal- or burglar-proof. Each church needs to work out the most appropriate solutions for its own situation, in discussion with local people, the police and the insurance company. But organs can have locked side panels and console doors, and the area round the organ can also be arranged to discourage nosy-parkers.

A certain amount of damage can sadly be caused by careless organ enthusiasts. Those with famous organs should be particularly careful of requests to examine their instruments; only serious students should be allowed access.

The organ section in the insurance policy should cover casual or accidental damage as well as total loss.

Environment

The main factors which affect the materials from which an organ is made are light, temperature, humidity, dirt, airborne pollution and animal attack. If the conditions are generally favourable, an organ can last for decades without attention. At their worst, they

fig. 4
An organ chamber with problems: a damp and crumbling wall in the north-west corner of the church, debris, careless painting, woodworm in the building frame (temporarily strengthened).

can mean a clean and overhaul every ten to fifteen years and a wholesale replacement of parts every twenty to thirty.

Light

Light levels in churches are usually low and cause a problem to organs only where direct sunlight shines on the case, bleaching the colour of the wood, or causing silk backing to the front pipes to deteriorate.

Heat

Organs are safer in a cool rather than warm space; it is better if the temperature does not drop below 5°C. They also tend to settle down to the temperature and humidity of the room, which should remain reasonably consistent. Heat becomes a problem for materials when accompanied by moisture and pollutants. Warm, humid air will encourage mould and fungi. When warm air is blown into a cold organ, water condenses onto any surface whose temperature is lower than the dew point of the air. This can cause electrolytic corrosion on action wires or metal pipe feet.

Humidity

Relative humidity (RH) is a measure of the amount of water that the air can hold, compared with the maximum it can hold at that temperature. The higher the temperature, the more water the air can hold, so as temperature rises in any given space, the drier the atmosphere, and vice versa.

Churches in this country usually suffer from damp rather than dry conditions. It is more important that the atmosphere is stable than to keep it to recommended museum humidity levels (45% to 55% RH). If conditions are damp (over 65% RH for long periods), the risks of mould, wet rot, failed joints, spoiled varnished surfaces, etc., increase. It may be too costly to lower humidity levels, but if an organ is in a damp church, it is a good idea to move it away from damp spots (often against north walls), so that local mould and bug attacks are avoided, and the air intake does not cause condensation inside the mechanism or pipes.

Good housekeeping

fig. 5
The effects of damp and inappropriate rebuilding: the backfall beam above has fallen into its constituent parts, and the beam below is an octave coupler inserted into a small early-nineteenth-century chamber organ.

If a building has been used to high humidity levels, it can be dangerous if the levels are suddenly lowered, as is the case when a new central heating system is installed. If an organ used to damp is dried out, the wood will shrink in a destructive way and crack, split and open joints. If the movement back and forth is repeated, materials which react to moisture in different ways will detach themselves, for instance the ivories of the keyboard.

Humidity levels can be measured most accurately with wet and dry bulb hygrometers. Dial hygrometers (which use the sensitivity of human hair to measure humidity) can be accurate but need regular re-calibration. Digital hygrometers are more convenient, but are not so accurate.

It is always worth taking measurements before a major restoration if there are reservations about humidity levels. It is possible to take preventive action which, though it costs money, may ensure that the restoration fund is money spent effectively.

Dirt

Grit, dust and general debris are often deposited in an organ as a result of carelessness, e.g. by repairing the church roof over the organ without first covering it or by over-enthusiastic spring cleaning. Generally speaking, the more a church is used, the more

Historic organ conservation

fig. 6
Organs without roofs leave their pipes exposed to foreign bodies.

fig. 7
Mouse damage on the front rail of a pedalboard.

dust will collect in the organ, particularly the fluffy kind. It helps to have some roof or lid over the organ, which will catch any grit which falls off the ceiling, as well as insects and bird excreta, etc. Most Victorian organs, however, were designed without roofs, intentionally, and either cannot or, for tonal reasons, should not be covered. After a period of years, all organs have to be given a professional clean.

Pests

Certain animals can become pests, especially if the conditions encourage them. They like dirt, damp, quiet and warmth. Woodworm is the greatest scourge. If it is rampant, only repeated fumigation will control it. Mice can cause irritation by eating keys or leaving droppings between them, and chewing bellows leather. Bats can cause damage to an organ case; bat urine stains are hard to remove.

Tuning and maintenance

If an organ is functioning perfectly, in a stable environment with an even temperature, it would never have to be tuned. But it is not a perfect world and fluctuations in temperature and humidity have to be expected. Tuning is an important process and needs attention by all concerned. Thought both by organ tuners themselves and by their customers about what constitutes good tuning will prolong the life of the organ.

The normal practice is to have the organ tuned a fixed number of times a year, according to the size of the organ and the funding of the musical life of the church. The frequency of the tuning is usually regardless of the environmental conditions of the church and around the organ, even though these may have a material effect on the tuning. In fact most organs should not need tuning more than once a year. For organs with metal flue pipes cut to length (i.e. cone-tuned), the tuning should settle down after two or three years of being checked right through. For organs with metal flue pipes tuned with tuning slides, much depends on the care with which the slides are made and fitted, but the chances of the tuning slipping is always greater, and will increase with the passing years.

The pitch of reed pipes does not change with the temperature changes, though it is affected in a random way by such hazards as dust, wool fibres and insects. They can be tuned and re-tuned without damaging the pipes.

Tuning visits

It is sensible to bring an organ completely into tune once a year, at a season when temperature and humidity are average. In other words it is better to arrange the contract so that the organ is fully tuned and its condition discussed rather than to have an occasional brief visit which merely corrects the worst faults.

Heating

An organ may be tuned throughout the summer, only to become unreliable in the winter through the effects of the heating system. For instance, a hot air heating system may be ideal for the congregation and its balance sheet but it can play havoc with the tuning and materials in the organ. If a heating system is only used for a short time, it will warm the air, but not the fabric of the church. It will also heat the body of the church first, and leave the corners, not to mention organ chambers, till last. The result is draughts, some of them highly localized, which can send one part of the organ out of tune with another, e.g. if the front pipes receive warm air before the inside pipes. Another effect can be stratification of the air temperature, so that organs with pipes on different levels can suffer pitch changes between departments.

On the other hand, a church with a type of heating which creates a comfortable temperature during the week can become extremely dry if the outside temperature falls below zero for more than three or four days. The tuning will remain satisfactory, but the wood will start to shrink rapidly.

Possible solutions include:

- a humidification system for the organ to prevent condensation or localized moist air;
- heating the church to a low temperature through the week and bringing it up to greater levels of comfort for services.

Inspections

Quite apart from annual tuning, it is advisable for organs to undergo a periodic inspection, when their condition can be assessed and congregations alerted to possible deterioration. It makes sense if this is allied to the quinquennial inspections of the overall fabric of the building. The form should be devised to allow someone with knowledge of the instrument, but not necessarily expert in its workings, to assess its condition and to suggest reasons why particular problems are occurring. For instance, if a pipe is not speaking, the report could indicate whether this was because

- the pipe is not in its hole;
- some dirt is hindering the wind flow;
- the pipe is damaged;
- the pipe has been pocketed by souvenir hunters;
- the key action has a fault, e.g. a broken link in a mechanical action, or a leak in the pneumatic action.

The inspection should:

a) check the specification and appearance and record alterations, e.g.:
   - the position of the organ and the console;
   - the specification on the console (builder's label, stop labels, method of stop control, key compass, type of pedalboard, accessories);
   - the appearance of the case (style, ornamentation and finish of case, finish of front pipes, key coverings).

b) check the overall condition of the organ:
   - the appearance, e.g. dust and dirt, worm holes or damp patches, corrosion, scuffing, pinholes and inappropriate electric fittings;
   - playing conditions, e.g. worn or missing key coverings, keys not moving or returning properly, touch depth;
   - tuning: play the Principal 4' in chords, and the principal chorus in single notes and in octaves.

c) check for dehydration, deterioration of materials, etc.:

- switch the wind on; is the blower noisy? is there obvious wind noise?
- pull a stopped 8' and play scales through the compass; do the keys feel uniform? do the pipes seem to receive enough wind?
- play scales through the compass for each stop; do they speak properly?
- pull a Flute 4' or Fifteenth; are there any murmurs before depressing a key (known as ciphers)?
- Try all the keys, consecutively and in simple chords; do any pipes other than those being played murmur (known as a running)? Another test for potential runnings is to depress an octave of keys at a time without pulling a stop; more than slight murmuring indicates a weakness.

d) check the environmental conditions of use and maintenance, e.g. heating system, hot air, radiators, etc.

chapter 8
Organ building practice

How not to do it

The aim of conservation and restoration should be to retain as much of the original material as possible, but the British tendency to be constantly dissatisfied with their organs has led to frequent tinkering, and what has aptly been referred to as the car boot sale approach to organ building.

The result is that our organ heritage is being eroded, not by storm, but by stealth. As an example of 'renovation' rather than 'restoration' and certainly not 'conservation', the following catalogue lists what happened in the early 1990s to a perfectly respectable and unaltered organ built by a provincial builder in a small parish church in around 1840.

Tonally, there appeared to be no obvious changes, though it is difficult to tell from the console because all the original ivory stop labels have been replaced with plastic. The front pipes have all been replaced with zinc replicas, and the reed tongues and

fig. 8
The use of inappropriate materials in the restoration of a mid-eighteenth-century windchest.

tuning wires are new. The metal pipes have all been bathed in a caustic solution and mopped. The wooden pipes have been planed down and oiled, the caps removed and screwed back. The reed resonators have been slotted, and the bass tongues loaded. The pipes had already been cut down and tuning slides fitted.

Unlike the casework, the console has not been stripped and oiled but the ivory overlay of the naturals has been replaced with a synthetic substitute, the stop labels replaced and departmental name labels added, the organ builder's label attached prominently on an otherwise anonymous organ, and all the switches and light fittings replaced in the latest plastic.

There is a new pedalboard. In the key action all the cloth bushing has been replaced, there are new trackers with phosphor bronze wires and plastic buttons, the roller arms have been cut open and plastic eyes inserted. The steel rollers have been repainted black, the rollerboard painted for the first time, in battleship grey. The pedal action has been replaced with electro-pneumatic.

In the chest, the upperboards have all been lifted onto Schmidt seals, the bearers packed up with hardboard, and the sliders replaced with synthetic material. There is a new bushed hole into each channel through the front rail of the bar frame. The upperboard and faceboard screws have been replaced. The pallets have been re-leathered with new paper on the grid and with felt on the pallets. The springs, pulldowns, pallet eyes and pallet guide pins have been replaced with new phosphor bronze wire with plastic inserts in the eyes. The brass pulldown strip has been replaced with nylon inserts. The inside of the pallet box has been painted red, and the outside painted brown. The swell box has been painted black on the outside and white inside, and all the shutter cloth has been replaced. The vertical rod has been replaced with aluminium tube, and the trigger swell pedal with a balanced one. There was already a blower, but the re-leathering of the bellows has been taken as an opportunity to remove the original feeders and pumping mechanism, and to paint all the bellows and trunking black.

The work is tidy, the craftsmanship competent, but the spirit of the original organ has been completely obliterated.

Towards good practice

There will always be a case for replacing rather than conserving, for restoring to full working order rather than leaving an authentic work of craftsmanship for posterity. Organs in different locations are going to demand different approaches; factors which create problems in one place may not in another. The case study quoted above shows the danger of a careless approach, not carelessness of action, for the craftsmanship was good.

The aim of restorers should be to do as little as possible. They need to ask: can the original parts be saved? If they are damaged, how much can be re-used? If the parts have to be replaced, is it possible to use the same material?

Paradoxically, re-using the old parts can take longer than discarding them; it requires a flexible approach and calls for an experienced craftsman. Some of the best continental workshops have separated their restoration departments away from those building new instruments and the most versatile and experienced workmen are employed in the former. It is much less time-consuming to supervise employees making a new organ than repairing an old one. Whereas instructions for a new rank of pipes can be given at the start of the work, in restoration each pipe can present a different problem, a special dilemma.

The old methods of 'restoration', which have been described here as 'renovation', were the solution of large workshops and factory units, with a division of labour to workmen trained in specialized areas. It is not surprising that a wholesale approach to each problem was adopted by management.

Modern conservation requires a flexible approach from responsible craftsmen equipped with a wide variety of craft techniques and able to assess the extent of wear or damage, and take the appropriate steps to remedy the faults with the minimum impact on the old material.

chapter 9
Deterioration of materials

General

All materials deteriorate. They last longest in ideal conditions. The problem with the organ is that it is made from a variety of organic and inorganic materials, not all of which benefit from the same environment.

Generally speaking, organic materials like a fairly humid environment, while metals, adhesives and certain finished surfaces like a fairly dry environment. Organic materials include leather, cloth, wood, parchment and paper. These will survive better in levels of relative humidity of 55% to 65%. Metals do not suffer in a dry environment, but will corrode faster when it is damp. Adhesives and polished surfaces do not appreciate damp, but do suffer when the atmosphere is too dry. The recommended range is 50% to 65% RH, though there are organs which have survived happily for centuries at levels up to an average of 75%.

Problems of wear and tear are more clear-cut, though not necessarily easier to control. There is probably, so far as the organ is concerned, an optimum amount of use by players. Particularly in damp environments, the mechanism should be used once a week, to keep the joints free. Historic organs with surviving historic actions, in museums for instance, should perhaps be used no more than that.

Organs which are in constant demand by students will wear out much faster than organs used once a week. It is likely that their actions will already have been replaced many times, but if they do still have a historic action, some kind of rationing system should be put in place. Constant usage by players, however, probably does less damage than constant attention from the organ builder. Frequent tuning, even by the most accomplished tuner, will introduce dirt into the organ, rub away at wooden edges, disturb paint work. Ironically, a full restoration project, with dismantling, transport to the workshop and re-assembly, may cause more minor damage than neglect. The best way to avoid the attentions of the organ builder is to ensure a stable environment, and as little disturbance to the organ as possible. It is a virtuous circle.

Wind

The organ is a wind instrument. All its parts are designed to contain wind, or to direct its flow in a particular direction. Organ wind is compressed only slightly (about 1% for each 100 mm of water pressure) but it is sufficient to cause leakage wherever there is an opportunity. As the wind is required for a musical, and not a purely physical, effect, any alterations to the wind system, however small, will change the character of the organ.

The advantage of wind over other sound producers is that it does not age, though the surfaces and edges over which it flows may have changed with time. The disadvantage is that alterations are not necessarily obvious. The wind pressure can be upset by removing or adding bellows weights. Even slight leaks, including bleed holes, lower the wind pressure.

Over the last 150 years, a revolution has been seen in the way wind is provided to the reservoir. Instead of a blower working gravity-fed wedge bellows, or feeders to a horizontal reservoir, almost all organs now have an electric blower with a cut-off valve, and often with concussion bellows and other devices to steady the wind. The result is that the wind is now much likelier to be steady than it would have been. However, the quality of the wind is unlikely to be the same, a factor increasingly recognized in restoration schemes.

Leather

Leather is used for the bellows, hinges and gussets, and for seals, at the pallet, trunk joints, slider runs, etc. Advances in leather technology have been responsible for some of the advances of the organ as a sophisticated musical instrument. Almost all the leather in surviving historic organs is sheep's leather treated with alum salt. It is almost always glued with animal glue. Where it is used as a hinge, it is likely to fail in its job more rapidly than when it is used as a seal. Most major restorations will involve a replacement of the bellows leather as a matter of course, and only in special circumstances will a particular effort be made to preserve it.

Organic materials contain moisture; as the relative humidity changes, so does the moisture content of the material. The shape and structure of the material can change and degrade. In the case of leather, especially the rather soft leather used in organ building, the fibres shorten with age, so that a material which can be pulled and stretched when new is easy to tear when old. Also, the surface flattens, and can no longer be teased up, as it can when new. It is difficult to arrest this process artificially; any treatment to stop the leather from absorbing moisture will also stiffen it or stop the glue penetrating it. Once leather has deteriorated, it cannot be revived.

This ageing process is encouraged by a dry atmosphere, and even more so if it is alternately dry and wet. The shortening of the fibres affects the porosity of the leather, so that an old bellows will deflate more quickly than a newly leathered one. The effects are also noticeable where leather is used as a hinge, so that along ribs and the corners of gussets the leather will crack and eventually split.

In damp conditions leather can attract mould, which can attack the fibres and shorten their life. Mould is encouraged by the use of flour, occasionally used as a cleaning agent, or like French chalk, to stop the pores of the leather. It does no good as either. Leather bellows also attract mice.

Cloth

Cloth is used for a soft landing (e.g. under the keys and the thumper rail) and as a seal (e.g. between swell shutters). In historic organs the cloth is usually woven, thick and with a raised nap. Felt became increasingly popular in the second half of the nineteenth century.

Cloth and felt can become clogged with dirt so that they lose their sponginess. Also, as with leather, the fibres shorten with age and use. Some of the life can be brought back into the cloth by cleaning it, either dry-cleaning with a vacuum cleaner, or wet-cleaning with a wetting agent (not a detergent).

The commonest enemy of cloth and felt used inside the organ is the larva of the common clothes moth. The moth likes to lay its eggs in slightly damp, enclosed spaces. A common treatment is to lay naphthalene crystals in the affected areas, under the keys and thumper rail, the back and front rails of the pedalboard, and between the material and the wood of the swell shutters. Infestation can be guarded against by vacuum-cleaning accessible areas of cloth.

Wood

Wood forms the material for many of the essential parts of an organ. The important parts of the mechanism depend on its properties and behaviour for their working. If the wood used in the keyboard, the bellows or the windchest is less than satisfactory, or subjected to unreasonable demands, then the organ will cease to execute its duties as it should. The organ also depends on wood for its appearance, and for some of its sounds.

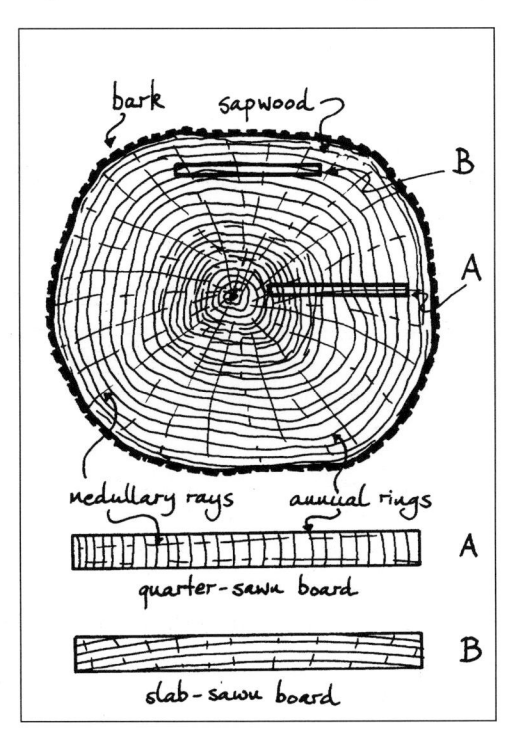

fig. 9
Section through an oak tree: quarter-sawn boards (A: radial) react half as much to moisture as slab-sawn boards (B: tangential) and ten times as much as the length of the board.

Wood is an organic material. Its hygroscopic nature means that it responds directly to changes in atmospheric humidity. It also has a strong directional grain. It expands and contracts across the grain, though not along the grain. Boards that have been cut on a tangent (i.e. along the rings of the tree) will be less sensitive to changes in moisture level than boards which are cut radially (across the rings). The former are known as slab-sawn, the latter as quarter-sawn.

The cell structure of wood means the response is irregular. If the humidity changes, the wood will respond more at some points than others, causing it to twist, bend and warp. An organ builder will therefore try to use wood that is as straight and regular as possible. It is, however, difficult to match wood bought today with the wood in historic organs, mainly because the quality of imported wood has declined. Good-quality softwood appears to be easier to acquire in continental Europe than in this country.

It is possible to use second-hand timber, though the cell structure of wood tends to degrade with time, leaving a material which breaks up at the edge of the tool. The process is slower with hardwood than softwood, and with finished wood than untreated wood. Recycled Victorian mahogany can often be the only solution to the problem of matching damaged mahogany parts.

The care involved in the use of wood starts with the drying process (seasoning). The wood used in organ building should have been dried out slowly and under the appropriate conditions. If it dries too quickly, the sapwood will dry out more quickly than the heartwood, and the open-grained parts more quickly than the more close-grained parts, causing splitting, twisting, bending and warping. The wood should have been selected for its suitability to the demanding applications required in most parts of the instrument. The workshop conditions should have been similar to those of the environment in which the organ is living so that the parts are not subject to sudden damp and drying out. A windchest made in the eighteenth century in a damp workshop for a chamber organ in a house with a relatively efficient heating system in a dry part of the country will have developed splits, just as will a similar organ moved today from a church to a centrally heated modern house. If a case is made in a dry workshop, and then moved into a damp church, the expanding panels can push the uprights away from the rails with a force which no glue joint can withstand.

As has already been described, wood can be bleached or split by direct sunlight. It can also be affected by various pests, of which fungi and woodworm are the most serious. Mould tends to feed on grease, oil and dust in or on the timber rather than the wood itself. Fungi will only flourish in a damp and poorly ventilated environment, which is usually to be found near ground level and in load-bearing members. Dry rot is rare in organs and does not usually advance far. Other kinds of rot can be treated by first curing the source of the damp and then treating with a wood preservative and strengthening or replacing the existing wood.

The woodworm will attack sapwood, fruitwood or softwood and enjoys animal glue, so reducing 1950s plywood to piles of dust. Oak and tropical woods are relatively immune. In continental Europe oak was for the classical period the pre-eminent organ building timber, and the survival of so many organs in such good condition bears testimony to its resilience.

It is the larvae of the beetle which cause the damage. The eggs are laid in cracks and splits, or on unfinished timber. In the spring the larvae will hatch and munch their way into and through the wood for about three years before emerging in May as adult beetles. They leave a freshly cut hole about 2 mm wide, usually with gritty sawdust called frass near it, the sure sign of an active worm.

The treatment consists of brushing a layer of colourless woodworm fluid on untreated surfaces. This forms a barrier which discourages the beetles from laying, and kills the emerging ones, though the larvae already enjoying the wood will carry on, a process which it is almost impossible to arrest. Polished wood can be treated by injecting through the holes.

Ivory and bone

Ivory and bone are used for key coverings, stop knobs and occasionally labels, and in the last hundred years or so for other console controls. Ivory has been used for natural or sharp keys from the seventeenth century, when white keys became usual. In Britain, bone has only been used in recent years, though it was the usual covering for white keys in continental Europe.

Both ivory and bone have a cellular structure with a directional grain. They are sensitive to humidity and heat, and can absorb moisture, stains and dirt. Grease from players' fingers attracts dirt and yellows the surface. Staining from coloured cloth is easily absorbed.

Keys should only be cleaned with water-based preparations if they are removed instantly. Water can cause cracking and warping. Washing-up liquid can leave an irritating film on the surface. Methylated spirits applied with cotton wool is the approved method, since the spirits evaporate quickly.

Ivory naturals do wear and discolour under the hands but these disadvantages should not be used as a reason to remove them and cover with plastic. If the ivories have worn through to the wood, they can be replaced by re-used coverings from redundant instruments.

Adhesives

In the great majority of historic organs animal glue was used to join wood and apply leather and material, although sometimes flour paste was used to apply paper, either to swell boxes or ornamental key fronts or labels, since animal glue will rise to the surface of the paper. It is only after the Second World War that a number of different glues have been used.

Today's restorer has a particular problem in reversing inappropriate applications of modern glue in recent restorations. When a chest is flooded with white PVA glue, it forms a film over the animal glue which was used by the original maker, or a previous restorer, but it does not mix or adhere. It may form an effective layer, but it is more likely to crack, since the responses to heat and humidity of the two types of glue are different. Strictly speaking, PVA glue should not be watered down, since the emulsion prepared by the makers will be upset. PVA glue size can leave a mess like chewed bubble gum.

Animal glue, however, can always be re-activated with heat and water, and an application of fresh glue will bond with previous layers. The restorer's expert acquaintance with animal glue is essential, for many of the problems of restoration are the result of glue joints failing, or of applying new material to surfaces already impregnated with animal glue. Animal glue joints fail in very humid conditions, or where there are repeated movements from damp to dry and back again. In these conditions any tension in the materials will cause the two surfaces to part. Joints can also fail if they have been attacked by mould, which is very rare, or by woodworm, for worm infestation often takes the form of galleries travelling up and down glue joints.

Pipe metal

Organ pipes are usually made of an alloy of tin and lead. Before about 1850, small amounts of other metals, such as antimony, bismuth and copper, were added, and there were usually traces of others. From around 1840, zinc was used increasingly for the larger pipes. In this century, copper has occasionally been used for front pipes. The speaking parts of reed pipes use brass, and in this century, phosphor bronze.

The melting point of lead is 327°C, that of tin 232°C. The melting points of tin-lead alloys are not on a straight line between the two. Fortunately for the pipemaker, the lowest melting point is 183°C at around 62.93%, the composition of solder. This relatively low temperature means that pipe metal is quite easy to solder.

The addition of metals like antimony and bismuth can lower the melting point further, making the sheets easier to cast, as well as contributing to hardening. Both tin and lead, and their alloys, are soft metals, which can be cut, planed and scraped, bent and formed. Our notion of strength leads us to suppose that the alloy is at its weakest when the highest percentage is lead. In fact, although the metal may be at its most ductile, it is also at its most stable. Most pipes in historic British organs before about 1850 were made from alloys of between 15% and 35% tin. At 17% the alloy is at its least stable. Alloys with 40% tin and above are quite stable. This explains why British pipework is liable to collapse at the tip and at the mouth, and why languids are liable to sag. Languids were, and are, made of high-lead alloys, with antimony, bismuth and copper added. Mouths were strengthened with small ears soldered to the side of the mouth.

There was therefore some point to the general reverence for spotted metal. Fine spotted metal tends to be cast from a tin-lead alloy with a 45% to 55% tin content. The increasing fondness of the Victorian organ world for spotted metal no doubt arose from the sometimes rather poor pipework made during the period of great expansion in British organ building in the 1830s and 1840s. Leaving the spotted surface unplaned was no doubt a way of showing the quality of the metal. In the classical period, the metal was almost always planed, but British pipe metal was never hammered. When replacing pipes in historic organs, it is important to use metal which is close to the original in alloy and treatment, even if we do not entirely understand the tonal effects.

The environment is rarely responsible for the deterioration of pipe metal, except under certain specific conditions. Where the pipes are in contact with oak rackboards or upperboards, the tannic acid can corrode the metal. Usually the organ builder burnt the holes to give them a coating of carbon. Sometimes the pipe feet or the wood were given a shellac coat where they came into contact with each other. Under certain conditions, air carrying corrosive agents can condense inside the pipes, reacting with the metal, which becomes brittle and loses its ductility and stability. It is advisable to analyse the (usually white) powder before treatment. It is always poisonous.

Treatment depends on how far the corrosion has advanced. Tin and lead and their alloys are protected by an oxide layer; the degree of darkness is a rough guide to the pipe's age. This layer should not on any account be removed (e.g. with caustic soda or boiling water). Quite apart from removing material from the pipe wall, it once again becomes subject to corrosion. Zinc and brass also form an oxide layer with time, though with zinc the process tends to continue, with more or less rapidity according to the conditions. The surface of zinc will tend to produce powder spots even through gilding.

Metal corrosion is usually an electro-chemical process, and can in theory be reversed, e.g. by electrolytic reduction, or stabilized, e.g. by the use of a resin coating to penetrate and protect brittle and absorbent partially-corroded metal. At the moment, pipes tend to be replaced or repaired in the same way as newer pipes would be. It would be more desirable to use methods of reversing the effects of corrosion, or of reinforcing the pipe, without replacing the original metal.

Most deterioration in metal pipes is caused by human agency. Careless planting and staying by the original builder can encourage the pipes to collapse. Careless or desperate tuning can have the same effect. Restoration involving handling of the pipes can do them more harm than decades of standing in the organ. They become liable to dents and scrapes, and horizontal storage can mean that they become oval. While pipes stand upright and are a perfectly formed cylinder, they are stable. Once they are dented, stand at an angle, or become elliptical in section, they are on the road to collapse.

Pipe metal may be an easy metal for the pipemaker to work; it is also easy to make alterations. If pipes are referred to as 'worn out', they have usually suffered repeated attention during rebuilds. Every time the metal is bent about, or suffers from the voicer's knife, its life is shortened. The desire to keep altered pipes is less than it is for pipes in original voice and condition. Both their appearance and their sound can be held against them. Pipes which have suffered from the effects of time and environment, are much more likely to be treated with respect than pipes which have suffered from carelessness and the vagaries of fashion.

Other metals

Brass and iron wire were used for pallet springs and key actions; in the last century or so, copper, phosphor bronze, and tinned wire have also been used. Iron or steel has been used for blowing, swell and shifting movement pedals, and those elements in the swell, stop and combination actions which require strength but no bulk. Iron, mild steel and brass are used for various fixings and

fig. 10
Corrosion of the tips of steel pallet springs, contrasting a spring in contact with mid-eighteenth-century spruce (less corroded) with mid-nineteenth-century yellow pine.

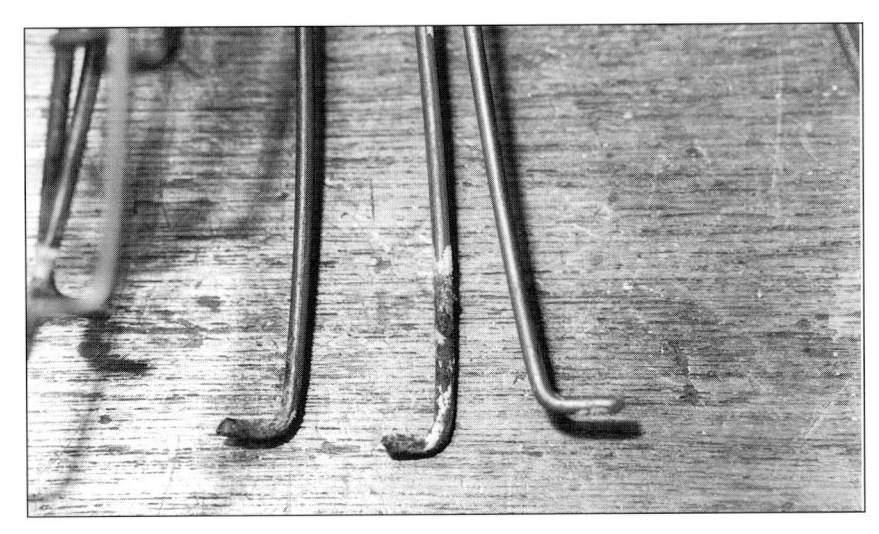

hardware, screws, nails, pins, hinges, etc. They can also be used for ornamental features.

All these metals acquire an oxide surface layer which protects them as well as any paint, though the conditions of warmth and damp which encourage corrosion can continue until the corrosion reaches unmanageable proportions. This is particularly true where they are in contact with materials which themselves contain corrosive agents, such as leather (tannic acid or salts), oak, or certain softwoods.

Metals can also attract corrosive agents when the air containing them condenses, which it is always liable to do when warm air comes into contact with cold metal. The drops of mildly dilute acid can cause corrosion on the surface. The worst instances are when two different metals are in contact with each other (e.g. brass tracker wires and iron roller arms), when the baser of the two metals corrodes as in a simple electric cell.

The processes of deterioration can be arrested if the environment can be changed, whether by changing the heating system, improving ventilation, or reducing local sources of moisture. If the metal has not been too badly affected it can be protected or simply cleaned and re-used. However, a functioning part which has been badly corroded may have to be replaced; a pallet spring half of whose thickness has disappeared is useless and has to be replaced (though the original should be kept with the instrument).

On the other hand, the protective layer of surface corrosion should not be removed, nor should it be covered with paint. The effects of corrosion can be significantly reduced by placing a barrier between the metal and the atmosphere or the wood. Screws should be lubricated with soap or a soft wax (not grease, which is supposed to break down the cells of the wood). Wire can be coated with a light wax.

All the metals used for action parts tend to work-harden (e.g. when bent and un-bent during assembly and removal to site), and to become brittle with age. Tracker wires should only be bent and removed with great care. If there are worries about damaging them, it may be possible to anneal the ends.

Exterior brass and metal fittings should not be polished to remove the patina. If the surrounding wood is waxed, the patina of the metal can be matched by going over it with the same wax polish.

Polishes, paints and varnishes

Historic cases have always been valued more highly than the instrument inside. Even so, their treatment has often been brutal. It is rare now to chop up the framework, but the desire to replace the finish is still with us. The result can be the loss of an old or original surface, and a historic case ends up looking like a modern replica. The finish of many of our seventeenth- and eighteenth-century cases has either been covered or stripped off.

Finishes only deteriorate for a reason. These can sometimes be environmental. A damp atmosphere can give clear polish or varnish a milky look, which can only be removed with warmth and elbow grease. Daylight bleaches out colouring. More frequently the damage is man-made. The light translucent varnish on Georgian cases was often covered with the opaque colouring of Victorian polish, which darkens and contracts at a different rate to the underlying surface, leaving a maze of little cracks. In this century a common approach is to strip paint and polish off the wood, leaving a light colour and a dry surface, and exposing cracks, damage and local discoloration. Movement around the organ can leave paint and varnish chipped, scratched or worn away. Consoles can be disfigured by pinholes, patches of Blu-Tack, or burns or splashes from wax candles.

The surface finish given to a case was intended to be permanent. In ideal circumstances it does not need upkeep or reviving. It should need no more than dusting with a good supply of clean dusters. The casework should not be buffed, or polished with wax. The usual result is a high degree of maintenance in accessible areas, and damage to fragile areas (veneers, carving, and mouldings). Under no circumstances use an aerosol spray, which can penetrate the surface of the original polish and leave a permanent film.

If deterioration has proceeded so far that repair work is needed, call a professional. Staining, painting and polishing furniture is a specialized business. However, it is also a conservative trade, and the techniques used to revive a surface are not always sympathetic to the existing one. Tests should be encouraged, and surface finishes should always be added to rather than stripped away. Do not strip away old finishes.

Gilding

Oil-gilding of front pipes and carving was very popular in the classical British organ. Almost all chamber organs of the eighteenth and early nineteenth centuries have gilded front pipes, usually non-speaking, sometimes made of metal but usually of wood. On dummy wooden pipes there will be a layer of gesso, a mixture of whiting and animal glue, then a layer of varnish on which the gold leaf is laid while the varnish is still tacky.

If left alone the gilding does not deteriorate, though it may get dirty. It will acquire a patina with age, though very slowly. The incongruous effect of new gilding means that original or old gilding should only be replaced when the original surface has lost all character. A skilled gilder can revive original gilding and blend in any patches of new work.

Any repairs should be left to the expert. Gilding can seem robust but it is easily damaged. If it is dusty, it should never be rubbed, for instance with a cloth, but cleaned with a soft brush, for instance of pony hair. Water should not be used but, if it has been, it should be allowed to dry naturally rather than being wiped off. Finally, never touch in gilding with gold paint, since it has a different texture and discolours differently. Gold paint has sometimes been mistakenly applied to provide a second coat. This should be removed by an expert.

chapter 10
Technical matters

Recording

All repairs and restoration projects should include a restoration report. If the organ is one of note, it should also have a survey of its design to assist builders, historians and restorers of similar organs. If time and money are pressing, the first priority is to make an inventory, then a photographic record, and finally, if a full report has been paid for, drawings and descriptions, with measurements.

An organ should always be recorded before it is dismantled, detailing parts which have been altered and are to be restored or which are likely to change during restoration, including RH (to be matched to the workshop or its new home), wind pressure, and pitch. A full photographic record is also desirable to obtain an objective account of the unrestored state, so that the restored organ can be compared. The restoration report should be lodged both with the church and with the providers of grant aid. It will prove most useful to the next restorer, who will thus be able to distinguish the work described from former repairs and to know how to assess their own intervention.

Church cleaning and building work

All too often repair work is carried out on an organ or a new organ is installed, only for the church to be filled with dust. If there is to be any repainting, building or spring cleaning, the organ should be wrapped in plastic with all the gaps taped. This is especially important if the organ is uncased, that is, is not covered with a roof. Dust can penetrate the smallest holes, or gaps in the plastic covering; for pipe organs, dust is the worst enemy, and particularly building dust and grit.

Try and persuade the congregation's cleaners to avoid using brushes and brooms, which disperse the dust, and use a vacuum cleaner, damp rags or mops. If a great deal of dust is created, use a spray to bring the dust down.

Acoustics

Organs benefit from a reverberation period, a sense of speaking into space which gives a bloom to the sound. The process of voicing to maximize this effect should be carried out in the church or at least adjusted in it once the organ is installed, so that the instrument achieves its best possible result for the building. Any changes to the interior or to the reflective surfaces will therefore affect the sound of the organ.

When there is a proposal for a new aisle or sanctuary carpet, pew runners or embroidered kneelers, tapestries or banners, the effect on the acoustics is rarely considered. It ought to be. Many churches that had adequate acoustics for speech and music have been made more difficult for speakers and singers because of considerations of comfort or ornament. In these days, when the speakers can be aided artificially, the music has to fend for itself. It should not be forgotten that a good church acoustic is the best stop on the organ.

Position

Anglican organs have moved from screens round the chancel (up to 1660) to the west gallery (up to 1850), back to organ chambers north of the chancel, and now tend to hover about within striking distance of the action near the chancel steps. If an organ is to be restored, the position for which its appearance and voicing were intended should be reinstated as well. An open position is as anachronistic for a Victorian organ designed for a chamber as a chancel position would be for a restored Georgian organ. This is not a matter of tonal suitability, but of the way in which the organ was designed to fit into the service.

From an acoustic and a visual point of view, an elevated position facing up the long axis of the church is by far the best. For most Anglican organs, the opportunity for optimal performance disappeared when galleries were removed in the years after 1850. It is true, though little appreciated, that money spent on restoring the position of the organ often improves the result more than if the equivalent sum were spent on restoration or enlargement. This is particularly true if the organ has been moved under the tower or into the chancel; even wide arches can cut off sound in a remarkable way.

Similar problems arise when there are plans for a re-ordering, whether an existing organ is to be retained or it is to be replaced by a new organ. The presumption should be that the organ stays put. If a change is considered, it should only be because the organ has been moved from its original position to an unsuitable one.

Size and stoplists

Whether an organ is in its original state, or has been rebuilt fundamentally but given a new integrity, its character should be respected and left intact. The stops of a historic organ should stay where they are, and the pipes should stay on their upperboard holes.

If an organ has been so altered that its character does not proclaim a particular period but nonetheless it contains elements of high quality, which survive from the last period when the organ formed an integrity, these elements should form the basis of the reconstructed instrument, e.g. by moving back transposed ranks or restoring re-voiced reeds.

As a general rule, pipes should stay where they are, or should move back to some place where they have stood before, as established by a well-researched scheme. For instance, if ranks have migrated from one part of the organ to another, or have been re-pitched a fifth or an octave, then they can be moved back again. Historic pipework should not be commandeered to form a reconstituted organ, unless the aim is a reconstruction of the original builder's intentions. If it is used in what is otherwise a new or rebuilt organ, its historical and musical authenticity will have been compromised.

Advisers and customers should beware of the migration or replacement of ranks of pipes behind an apparently unaltered stoplist. A reputable organ builder accredited for historic restoration is not going to exchange a stop for an inferior one in his store, but it has been common practice in the past, and may still continue in some quarters.

Pitch and tuning

Pitch

The pitch used today is a^1 = 440Hz at 15°C. This will rise or fall by approximately one Hz (Hertz or cycle per second) for a rise or fall of one degree centigrade, but nominally every new instrument built in England will have this pitch. In the past, however, pitches varied. Byrd, Purcell or Handel would, in their times, have known organs built at two or three different pitches, according to the time at which they were built, the builder who built them, and whether they were church or chamber instruments. Even in Victorian times, the major builders used different pitches. In 1878, the pitches taken from the standard pipes of different London workshops varied from A436 at Bishop to A445 at Willis. Concert hall organs were about half a semitone sharper.

The problem is not critical with church organs. Professional singers know there is something wrong when the pitch is not where it should be, but for ordinary mortals it matters no more now than it did in Victorian England. Pitch only becomes contentious when the organ plays with other instruments, that have their own fixed pitch. As a result, some chest and chamber organs are now built with a facility for changing pitch to correspond to the pitch of modern baroque instruments.

In the few instances where a historic pitch, or the evidence for it, has been preserved, a way should be found of keeping the evidence. Organ pipes, unlike most other musical instruments, give fairly reliable evidence for historical pitch. Pipes should not be lengthened or cut down, though the addition of tuning slides can sometimes be an acceptable compromise. The tuning slots and windows at the back of front pipes should not be tampered with, unless a slit can be made which preserves the earlier evidence.

Tuning

Almost all organs have at some time been re-tuned to equal temperament, which makes the few untouched examples of earlier tuning systems all the more precious. Most of the larger firms switched to equal temperament in the 1850s and 1860s, but some firms and tuners retained older tuning systems for longer, and some organs were simply never re-tuned to the new system. However, if an organ has always been tuned in equal temperament, it should not be altered. Current tastes in tuning are not appropriate just because they are more 'historic'.

Repairing and restoring pipe tops

If the pipes are still cut to length and coned fiercely one way and the other, suspect an alteration of a previous tuning system. For instance, if all the C sharp pipes have been sharpened (coned out) or the B flat pipes flattened (coned in), this is a sign that equal temperament was not the original tuning. The tuning could be revived, though an assessment of the state of the pipe tops should be made before they are straightened out and re-coned, a process which can make the metal brittle and shorten its working life. If the metal pipes have already suffered the effects of vigorous cone-tuning, they will have weakened and buckled at the mouth, the foot will have bent and the toe crushed into the upperboard hole. Whatever the scheme, the pipes should never be cut down.

The following tuning methods should be considered:

1. The pipes can be tuned out of the organ, which is time-consuming but imposes much less strain on the pipes than tuning them in the organ. Slits, splits and cracks can be soldered, and the solder seam thinned down, but since the new solder is harder than the old metal, hitting it with the cone will impose too great a strain.

2. Consider switching to tuning slides, rounding out the pipe tops and leaving the pitch slightly flat, particularly if the tuning is not stable. Tuning slides on old pipework must be carefully made if they are to grip the pipe without distorting it, or scraping the walls.

3. The pipes, particularly the larger ones, could be pinch-tuned by bending over the top edge of the pipes by hand, a method known from old organs abroad. It is an untidy and laborious method and repeated bending of the metal can tear the tops but it imposes no strain on the rest of the pipe.

4. For larger pipes, a slit can be cut with shears, and the metal bent in or out, a method used for front pipes in early organs. This is preferable to tuning rolls on old pipework, where the metal is too brittle to accommodate much bending. Most classical English organs had all their pipes cut to length, without tuning rolls. Slits were used increasingly during the eighteenth century for front pipes at least.

5. If a reed resonator is too long, a slit at the top will shorten it without removing evidence of the original pitch.

6. Where pipes have been slotted at a later date, the slots should be soldered up and the pipes tuned to their original length, if it still exists.

If the pipes have already lost their original lengths and have been cut down for tuning slides, there is nothing to preserve but there are other matters to consider:

1. If the pipes are fragile, or if there are no funds to lengthen all the pipes (especially if many of them are wooden), then the existing pitch and tuning should be kept.

2. It is acceptable to keep the tuning slides or to replace them if corroded, although they and the tuning knife tend to scrape and mark the sides of the pipe.

3. It is also possible to extend the pipes with new (or, for the sake of appearance, old) metal. In the writer's opinion, the tuning is much more likely to be stable if the pipes are cut to length, but there is the disadvantage that the solder seam is likely to be harder than the metal.

4. If the pipes are fragile, they can be tuned without strain by being cut to pitch and left, a course which is often sufficient if

sufficient care is taken in cutting down and thorough tuning at the first annual tuning visit. If they have to be coned, they can be taken out of the rack and tuned in the hand.

All organs, and not just historic ones, are better off if they are tuned as little as possible. In some places the environment does not favour stable tuning, though frequent tuning is not likely to help the situation. Usually, a tune through once a year is more effective in the long term than quarterly tuning of the most out-of-tune pipes. Electronic tuning machines can help by providing a reference point against which the tuning is judged, so that out-of-tuneness is not chased from pipe to pipe.

A restorer must weigh up all these factors and then proceed with great care. No organ is proof against tuners who are careless and impatient, or customers not prepared to pay for adequate maintenance.

Pipework

Metal pipes

If metal pipes are in bad condition with collapsed feet and mouths, or torn tops, they should be left to a pipe maker experienced in restoration. If a non-specialist is involved, care must be taken to remove the pipes from the organ in order, and to store them in such a way that there is no possibility of mixing them up. Metal pipes should be stored in trays in single layers; otherwise they will roll about or scrape against each other. Larger pipes are better stored upright, because they tend to become oval if left horizontal for long periods, but they need to be put in special racks with blocks for their feet. If they lean against each other the accumulated weight can have as bad an effect as leaving them horizontal. Similarly, if their toes are not positioned in a cone, the weight of the pipe can flatten the toe.

Pipes should be carried and transported with great care. More damage in the way of dents, scrapes and stubbed toes can be caused by a few days' handling and transport than during the previous decades standing in the organ. Pipes should not be re-marked unless their position is unclear. If they are re-marked, do not cover older marks.

fig. 11
Collapsed pipe foot (the result of inadequate racks and stays) and settling toes.

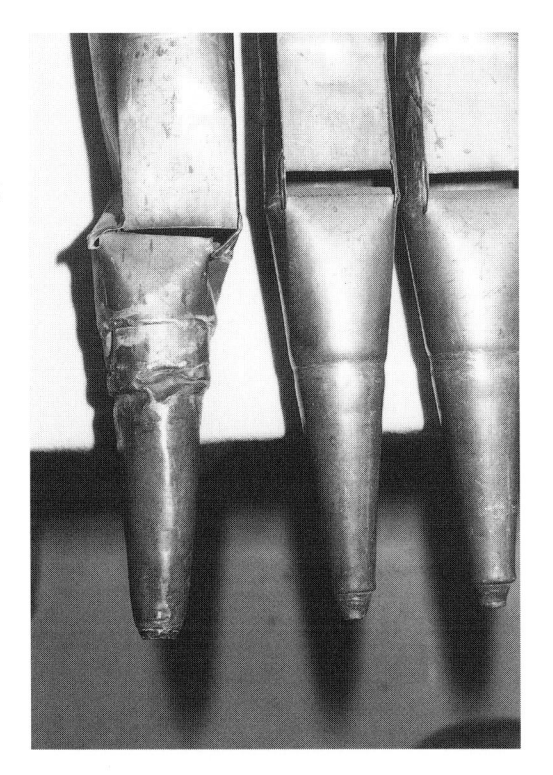

The patina should not be removed by washing and especially not by washing with caustic or boiling water or even washing-up liquid. Apart from losing the apparent age of the pipes, the removal of patina exposes the pipe to further oxidation. Metal pipes should be blown through, perhaps with compressed air, and tenacious dust carefully removed with brushes.

Restoring damage and deterioration

Minor dents and deformation have no effect on the sound or stability of a pipe and can be left. Usually dents are removed because of a concern for appearance rather than for an improvement in speech or tone. If one is trying to preserve the tuned length of a coned or stopped pipe, dents may have to be ignored. Today's dent can, however, become tomorrow's collapsed pipe. If the feet need repairs because toes have sunk into upperboard holes or the pipe is falling over, they should be sawn open above or below the rackboard level, reshaped, perhaps strengthened, and re-soldered. Sometimes disarranged tops can only be sorted out around a mandrel. Oval and misshapen pipes

Historic organ conservation

figs. 12 and 13
Pipe metal corrosion, caused by sulphur dioxide emitted by coal fires condensing inside the pipe feet below the rackboard.

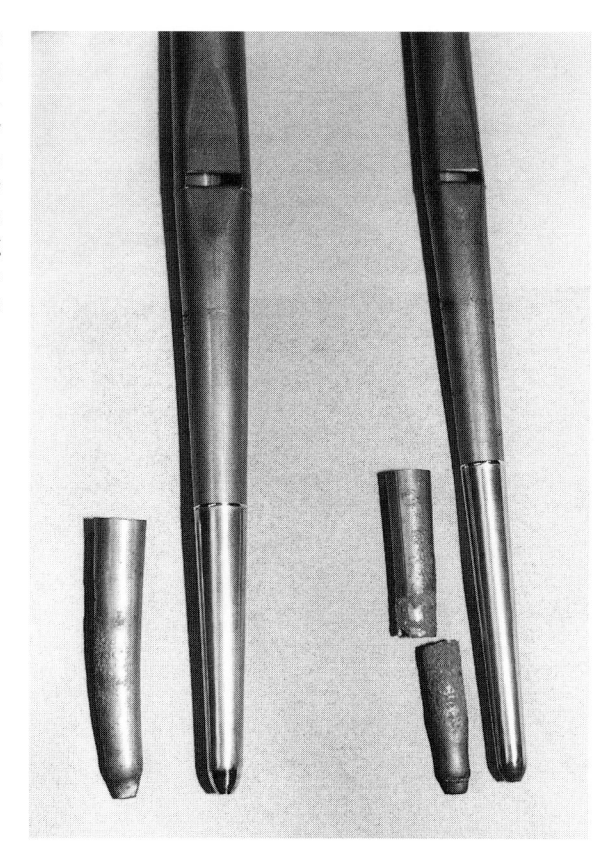

fig. 14
Efflorescence of impurities from the cast metal of a reed block.

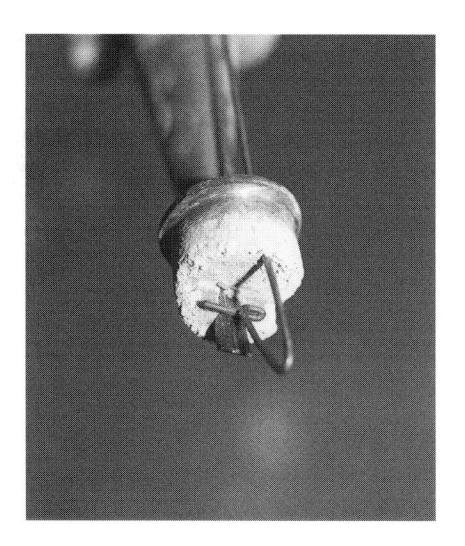

often have defective speech and tone. If pipes do have to be rounded out, great care should be taken not to disturb the upper lip or the languid.

Only rarely should the speaking parts of the pipe be disturbed. This can be justified when they have already been altered, and interference is the only way in which they can be restored. Re-soldering a pipe where the languid has come loose, or the mouth and languid have been disarranged and torn, is one of the special skills in restoration. Old metal at least has the advantage that it is easy to solder, since the oxide layer acts as a size. Even so, restoration of old pipework is inevitably a painstaking business.

Restoring alterations

Alterations to metal pipes are of two sorts; bending the metal, and cutting it. The former is more insidious because it is less obvious, though more easily corrected. The latter is easier to see but more difficult to correct.

The size of flues and toeholes may have to be changed during the regulation of speech and volume. That is quite straightforward if only one or two have been changed, leaving the remainder as a standard for comparison. A wholesale change is more controversial. There is no doubt that toeholes tend to get smaller with time and changes in taste, compressing into their upperboard

fig. 15
The painful results of over-zealous cleaning.

holes. Increasing voicing problems are often met by making pipes quieter. During the last century there has been a tendency to close toeholes and raise wind pressures, so it is tempting to reverse the process and lower the wind pressure and open toeholes to bring life back into the sound.

Some of the most vexing problems of restoration occur with pipes that have been altered with the knife. If the mouth heights have

fig. 16
The combination of soft metal and increasingly desperate tuning.

been raised, a judgement has to be made concerning whether the effect is bad enough to warrant restoring the original mouth heights. An experienced pipe maker should be able to solder in metal down to the correct level. If the body is sawn off above the languid, the ears and the alignment of the upper and lower lips may be lost.

Often the nicking of the languid has been deepened or extended to the lower lip and a judgement has to be made whether it is serious enough to try to reduce the effect. The nicks can be rubbed from below with a voicing rod, particularly if the foot has been sawn for reforming. Although not perfect, this method has some effect but often the removal of nicking leaves the pipe worse off than before.

Wooden pipes

Wooden pipes are more robust than metal pipes and more difficult to re-voice surreptitiously, but they provide their own problems. The most serious are warping and splitting blocks, caps and pipe walls, shrinking tuning stoppers, and failure of the glue joints. If a wooden pipe does not speak properly, it is more likely to be the result of escaping wind than of a fault in the voicing.

Restoring damage and deterioration

If the wood has at some stage dried out, the side walls may have shrunk away from the front of the block or, in larger pipes, the front of the block may become curved. In both cases, the cap either becomes loose, or is pulled towards the block, so that the flue changes shape, and wind escapes. If the walls have shrunk and taken the front wall, and therefore the upper lip, behind the face of the block, the pipe will cease to speak properly, if at all. If the boards are wide, and the rings are tangential to the heartwood, the walls may cup and pull away from the block. Sometimes splits appear in the upper lip, though damage to the lip, curiously, can have less effect on speech and tone than loss of wind.

If the humidity levels have returned to the original level, it may be sufficient to glue the pipe back together, but if the walls have shrunk too much it may be necessary to take the pipes apart and add wood to restore the width. The restoration of a rank in this condition is likely to be a lengthy and painstaking process. If the walls have shrunk a little, it may be sufficient to build them up with card, till the surface is flush with the block, and then glue the cap in place. If the pipe will not speak with the upper lip behind the block, it is preferable to remove the front wall and build up the sides, rather than shave away the front of the block, which will also remove the bevel and the nicking on the top edge of the block.

Failure of the glue joints is the result either of extreme dryness or of damp over a few weeks or of alternate dryness and damp at a less extreme level. In churches, damp is more likely to be the culprit. Animal glue joints can be re-activated with heat and water. If, as is common, the walls have split away from the top, they can be prised apart with a knife, and glue introduced with card. They should not be bound with tape or thread, which can obscure the pipe marks and damage the corners of the pipe. Screws and nails tend to rust after a time, split the wood and pose a problem for the next restorer and should be rejected in favour of wooden nails or dowels.

In theory, animal glue is the most reversible of adhesives. Even so, taking a pipe apart is a tricky business. Too much moisture or heat will deform the wood. The best method is to apply a fairly gentle level of heat and then hot water, alternately. Obviously great care has to be taken in re-gluing the wall to its original position, particularly if it is a front wall, or the process will not yield the desired results. Much restoration is a struggle with previous bad repairs.

The surface should not be planed down or painted. The appearance of the pipes is altered, all feeling for their age is removed, their history is lost through the removal of all the marks and there is no increase in durability as compensation.

If the stoppers have not been lubricated with grease or black lead, they should be left unlubricated. Grease is only a short-term remedy for easing sticky stoppers, whereas untreated leather and smooth pipe walls can carry on for decades. It may be necessary to replace decayed leather.

Restoring alterations

If the pitch has been raised, or the pipes moved up a space or two, the pipes will need lengthening. Obviously that is more time-consuming with wooden pipes than with metal. The pitch can be left as found, especially if there are qualms about taking more material off the top of the pipe walls. Small pipes can be lengthened with gesso (a mixture of whiting in animal glue), painting the mixture onto a greased stopper and planing it flat once the last coat has built the walls up. But usually the walls will be lengthened with wood, probably in the way that a mitred pipe would be straightened out.

Mouth heights can be restored, if the effect of raised cut-ups is offensive, either with wood or gesso. A slip of wood with a greased surface (or with polythene attached to it) is inserted into the pipe up to the block, and held in place with wedges. Either gesso is painted on and cut away afterwards, or a slip of similar wood is glued on, using a scarf joint. These operations are very time-consuming and expensive. Nicking of the face of the block can be filled with animal glue, gesso or silicon rubber, but it often makes little difference to wooden pipes and can be left.

Toehole wedges that look old should be left. A quiet pipe may well be quiet for reasons other than the wedges: e.g., such as wind leaks, a deformed mouth or a loose stopper. If the volume has to be regulated from pipe to pipe, the toehole wedges are the one easily altered area of the voicing in wooden pipes. As with metal pipes, alterations should only be carried out with great deliberation, bearing in mind the balance between regulating up to the loudest pipe or to a mean.

Voicing

Do not alter the voicing unless the validity of the alterations is clearly established. There should be no 'tonal re-balancing', and no preconceptions about the sound of the organ. During regulation of the pipework, alterations should be made with constant reference to the other pipes, so that the aim is to make them all alike, in the proportion that one would expect from the rank when new.

Do not depart too far from the existing voicing, especially the flues, toeholes and upper lip positions, which are easy to change. If the later alterations are obvious, a restorer familiar with the original builder's work may feel confident enough to reverse them, referring to other examples of his work.

Reeds

The number of reed stops in original condition is so small that they should be preserved at all costs. There are reasons for their rarity. Taste in reed tone has changed more frequently than it has in any other area of organ sound. Reed stops are by their nature more fragile than flue stops. And there are only a small number of reed voicers or even organ builders capable of regulating or repairing them. Even when they have survived they are often incomplete. The fashion for smoother tone has resulted in the loading and replacement of tongues, the replacement of shallots and alterations to the resonators, usually slotting. The fashion for indiscriminate replacement has meant that tuning wires and wedges also tend to be replaced. Nevertheless, a well-designed reed requires very little maintenance, nor do they 'wear out'. There are reeds in British organs still working with all their original parts which are 150, 200, 250, 300 years old. As with flue pipes, it helps if they are tuned and regulated as little as possible.

Restoring damage and deterioration

If reeds are to remain stable, they should be kept free from dust or dirt, whether in a case or hooded. Victorian reeds tend to survive better in swell boxes than on open chests, so long as the cloth on the shutters is not disintegrating. It requires very little to stop a treble reed from working. An eyelash is sufficient. If a reed is erratic in speech and tone, the solutions will probably require a specialist voicer or pipe maker, but problems associated with dirt and dust can sometimes be solved by the general organ builder.

Reeds should also be securely assembled. The loose bass resonators should fit the sockets, the blocks fit the boots, the shallots fit the blocks, the wedges hold the tongue and the wires move freely and evenly against the tongue. The more firmly the resonators are held in their stays, the better.

Most problems of speech or tuning are the result of dirt. If the dirt is obvious, tap the resonator against the hand, pull the tuning spring up to the wedge and blow across it, or carefully slide a piece of paper between the tongue and the shallot. If the dirt is not obvious, a magnifying glass may well reveal a hair or a minute piece of wool under the tongue. If the pipe is sharpened, that is, if the tuning spring is tapped down, but the tone and pitch hardly change, then the tongue is being pushed down by the spring, and the tuner should stop. Only those with some experience of handling reeds should attempt to put a tongue back, or remove the tuning spring from its face. If the pipe is silent, and dirt is not a problem, then a specialist should be called in. A common fault is the result of the tuning spring being pushed off the end of the tongue, and then pulled back up underneath it, introducing a fatal kink.

Reed voicing is the most difficult as well as the most rewarding part of the organ builder's art. Few are experienced in setting reeds up properly. Those who are not may be capable of straightening collapsed resonators and making loose parts fit, of adjusting tuning springs and fitting new wedges, but they should be discouraged from cleaning the surface of tongues and the faces of shallots, replacing tuning wires as a matter of course, cutting boots down or drilling holes in them.

As has been stressed above, the pipes should not be dismantled unless absolutely necessary. The more frequently they are removed, the more likely they are to become loose and difficult to tune. A loose shallot can be fixed by pinching the lead of the block against the sides of the shallot, or by gluing paper round the shallot, but it will never be as secure as it was to start with. Wedges will eventually disintegrate, and tongues work their way down the shallot. Tongues can be cleaned slightly by rubbing on a piece of card, but any abrasive will start to remove the curve.

Restoring alterations
Restoring an altered reed to an earlier state is the job of a specialist. Not only does it require someone with expertise in the

craft, it also requires a knowledge of the style of the original pipes. Changes of pitch and of resonator length have a disproportionate effect on reeds. If the pitch of the flue pipe is raised, the pipes may hardly speak. If the resonators have not been cut down, an acceptable method of achieving the effect without reducing the length is to cut a slit. If the pitch is lowered, the pipes become brash and brassy. Then the resonators have to be lengthened which with conical resonators is a time-consuming business.

If slots have been cut in pipes which were not originally slotted, the slots should be soldered up, though usually the slot is accompanied by a change in the tongues, which may also be loaded, and the shallots, which will be shorter and with a smaller opening. Such alterations are common in reeds made before 1880. Reversing these alterations is possible, but amounts to fashioning a new reed. An unaltered example will be required as a model.

It need hardly be said that historic reeds which seem to be unaltered in their voicing should not be altered, but should be cared for lovingly. Do not slot unslotted pipes. Do not load unloaded tongues. Do not replace shallots. Do not put flaps on open Oboes and Clarinets. Do not hood straight resonators. The same care should be taken with Edwardian reeds. Do not remove the leather from leathered shallots. Do not solder slots or open soldered lids.

Windchests

The difference between an overhaul and a major restoration is often caused by the amount of work required to make the windchest work. If the windchest is sound, then repair work is usually a matter of cleaning and adjustment. If it is not, then it usually has to be dismantled, which means removal to the workshop and some major surgery, including replacement of the pallet leather.

The function of the chest is to store and distribute wind to the pipes. If the chest has splits in the wood, failed joints or leaky leather seals, it cannot do its job properly. The main problem with making, testing and repairing windchests is that the element they contain, i.e. wind, is invisible. Sometimes the physical evidence for escaping wind is obvious. It may be audible, in which case it can be detected with a length of tubing, one end held against the ear, and the other end against the area of the suspected leak; or it may be visible, perhaps in the form of splits in the table of the bar frame, or gaps between the pallet leather and the bars. Unfortunately, the former only helps where the leak is escaping from the chest or trunks, of all leaks the least serious and the easiest to repair. The latter may indicate more serious problems but can often be relatively easily fixed.

Slider chests

In a slider chest, the serious leaks are those that occur between the pallet leather and the bars, within the bar frame, between the table, sliders and upperboards, and within the upperboards. Much of this leakage can be virtually invisible, although an endoscope can be used to explore channels, pallet hinges and grooves.

It is an advantage if the organ is functioning before it is restored. The chest can then be tested at the keyboards with the wind on. If a stop is pulled and no keys are played, but a note or murmur sounds, there is a cipher. If a stop is pulled, a key played, and a neighbouring note sounds or murmurs, there is a running. The most obvious sign of problems are small bleed holes punched into the leather covering the channels behind the pallet box, or in the feet of the flue pipes.

Ciphers and runnings

It may be possible to rectify a cipher without too much trouble. It may be caused by a key not returning properly, either because some dirt has fallen between the keys, or because a rise in humidity causes it to bind on the front guide pin. In the latter case the key may be freed in the short term by rubbing the key against the pin. It may be that there is a piece of grit on the pallet leather. Sometimes the grit will fall off if the key is touched repeatedly. If the pallets are accessible, and the open pallet can be illuminated, the grit can be rolled off the leather with a nail file, but the pallet should not be opened more than the key would open it, and the leather should not be roughed up. If none of these remedies solve the problem, it is likely to be a leak at the pallet hinge, a misshapen pallet or an uneven surface on the bar frame, which are likely to require the removal of the baseboard

A running does not usually have a short-term remedy, unless its cause is at the slider, in which case raising the humidity in the organ may have some effect. If the running is very local, say between two notes, then it is likely to be a failed joint, or a split across a bar. If there are patches of runnings between notes through the compass, these problems may have become general through the chest, or there may be splits in the table of the bar frame. If the stops are loose, and there are gentle whimpers over a large area of individual stops, it is likely to be a loose slider. Try playing an octave at a time with the stops off, and if there are murmurs in that octave it is quite likely to be wind pushing the slider up. Runnings are most likely to affect those pipes which speak with the least wind, and wind may cross a bar through a split connecting holes of another stop than the one whose slider is drawn. If the running is on one stop and one note, the problem may be in the upperboard.

fig. 17 Ciphers and runnings: a front rail shrinks away from a bar (pallet removed).

Technical matters

fig. 18
Runnings: the shrinkage of table and front rails pulls them away from the bars.

fig. 19
Runnings: the shrinkage of the table results in splits and failed joints (middle bearer in picture removed).

As a result of these uncertainties, the organ restorer has a repertoire of remedies which are usually applied wholesale, in the hope that the leaks disappear. Sometimes the faults may be cured, sometimes improved but not completely cured, sometimes the improvement is short-lived. Besides, the actions of the restorer are often more intrusive than the faults warrant, particularly if the repertoire of the restorer includes slider seals, bleed holes and the replacement of original parts. The ambition of the restorer should always be to make a reliable repair, whilst retaining as much of the original work as possible. For the windchest, more sophisticated methods of diagnosis and more precisely targeted surgery should be possible in the future.

In the meantime, common sense can reduce the traumatic effects of restoration on historic parts:

1. Always plan a dismantling so that the pieces return to the same place. That includes upperboard screws, rack pillars, pallet springs and pulldowns.

2. Do not dismantle unless it is warranted by the extent of the ciphers or runnings, i.e. the causes are more than short-term. On the other hand, do not be satisfied with a chest punctured with bleed holes.

3. Do not re-leather the pallets unless necessary, i.e. make an assessment whether the existing leather will last for another fifty years.

4. Do not include felt when re-leathering old pallets, unless it is original. Felt may make the action quieter, but as an aid to wind-tightness it is no substitute for levelling the surface of the pallets and the bar frame.

5. Splits in the table of the bar frame are always problematic, especially where the table has also lifted from the bars; routing a groove and filling with strips of the same wood is a more reliable long-term solution than pegs.

6. Joints which start to fail can cause particular problems in the classical method of chest construction, with separate pieces of wood and no joints; flooding the channels with the same type of glue that was used to make the chest is the only solution, with the extent, method and the sequence suiting the degree of the failure in the chest.

7. Do not replace the pallet springs or pulldowns unless the corrosion is advanced enough to affect the tension. If there is no more than a general coating, they could be dipped in hot wax or oil and left.

8. Do not replace the brass pulldown strip or pulldown purses. The latter are rare enough that they should be patched rather than replaced.

9. Do not use slider seals, do not groove the table or upperboards unless already grooved, do not make existing ones deeper, do not remove leather slider runs, do not graphite unless already graphited; in all these cases make adjustments to the bearers and flatten the table and upperboard surfaces to overcome the problems.

Key action

Keyboard

Nobody who sends away keyboards to be 're-conditioned' should become involved with a historic organ. The keys are the most sensitive part of an action, and are the point of contact for the player. The experience of performing on them should be one of the chief determining characteristics of any organ.

1. Do not be tempted to change or alter the keyboards to accommodate a larger key compass. Such changes are rarely necessary, especially as they tend to go out of date and do violence throughout the organ.

2. Do not replace ivories unless they are chipped or worn through to the wood. Even then, label the old key coverings and keep them inside the organ.

3. Do not use abrasives or buffing wheels, which can destroy the surface of the ivory. If the ivories are very yellow or translucent, it may be possible to use daylight to refresh their appearance.

4. If guide pin holes or pivot holes are loose, wood can be pieced in and re-drilled, or slips of wood can be inserted into the slot and re-filed. This is a more conservative solution than

using larger pins. Do not use bat pins. Do not bush unbushed keys with cloth.

5. Do not replace the original pedalboard with an 'up-to-date' one, especially where it was not made to be removable. An unusual pedalboard is a nuisance to newcomers but becomes familiar to the regular organist.

6. Worn pedal keys, especially naturals, will have to be pieced to restore their original height, but they should not be planed up, nor should unvarnished pedal keys be varnished.

Action

Whatever the type of action, do not be tempted to improve it, let alone replace it. An action which has been played for a hundred years does not suddenly become unplayable now. Similarly, an action which has lasted a hundred years can be made to last another hundred.

There may be exceptions, where a later alteration has made life difficult and a choice has to be made between the original action and the alteration. A patent twentieth-century action may prove impossible to adjust or repair, let alone restore. But generally speaking, cleaning and adjustment can help even an apparently heavy Victorian action to become playable. A player can become accustomed to an action which seems heavy to us. If a heavy action encourages judicious use of couplers, so much the better.

- When dismantling, make sure that everything can be returned to the same place; historic organs are often not as uniformly made as modern ones.
- Do not introduce modern aids to the touch weight, or alter ratios, though original pneumatic helpers should be restored. Often an action has been worsened by a later alteration (e.g. change of compass), in which case reversal of the alteration is preferable.
- Do not replace old trackers, stickers and wires. Do not put more adjusting points into old actions. Replace but keep old tracker wire buttons.
- Do not bush an unbushed action. Do not replace cloth bushes or washers unless the original ones have started to

Technical matters

disintegrate, in which case store them under the organ. If roller pins rattle in their holes, and squares are insecure on their wires, use wire of a slightly lower gauge and keep the old ones under the organ, labelled.

- Occasionally old techniques have to be re-learnt, and old types of tool and jig made new, a process with which the Institute of British Organ Building and the British Institute of Organ Studies should assist. An example is the leather bushes in the roller arms of Victorian organs, which require eyelet pliers.

- Do not paint metal parts. In historic organs, action parts were only ever painted for appearance, and there is no good argument for hiding the actions of the original builder under another layer. If it seems necessary, the environment is probably too damp in any case. Light oil and wax are short-term solutions.

- Most pneumatic actions are usable, and some are excellent. They should only be replaced or adapted if experience has shown that it is not worth the often considerable efforts the restoration of a pneumatic action can involve. The usual faults are loss of wind pressure through perishing of the motor leather and leakage at the connection, and corrosion in the moving parts. Leather work should usually be replaced.

- Preservation of the earliest electric actions and of some of the more experimental pneumatic actions seems quixotic, but it would be a pity if an example of each type were not kept.

Stop action

The main threat to the survival of a stop action has been the gradual development of registration techniques in the last 150 years, starting with angled stop jambs, and ending with electronic aids. Historic stop actions may seem inconvenient to modern players, but they do not themselves degrade to the point where replacement is necessary. If the stops are stiff or loose, then the fault is likely to be on the chest, where the sliders will need adjustment, either by altering the packing on the bearers, or by rectifying movements in the timber of sliders, upperboards or the table of the soundboard.

The commonest fault in the stop action is that pivot points have become loose, and there is too much lost movement at the stop knob. If that is the case, then the holes will have to be plugged and re-drilled, or the pins replaced. The pivot points should not be greased, which is bad for the wood, attracts dirt and tends to harden.

As with the key action parts, there is no point in painting the metal parts, since paint was applied purely for appearance. In those parts where a clean surface matters, e.g. trundle pivot pins, lever pivot pins, connections between shanks or rods and trundle arms, it is essential to have a good fit without paint or grease storing up problems for the future.

Historic combination actions and the combinations themselves should be left intact. They are essential pieces of evidence for past practice, and in most situations still provide the essential registrations.

Console

The console transmits the character of the organ to the player. The surroundings are important, as well as the physical characteristics. Consoles should not be made more comfortable at the expense of the original material. Organists should be protected from splinters but should learn to live with lesser difficulties such as wider stretches to pedal keys, short natural heads, awkwardly placed swell levers, or lack of department labels.

The controls at the console should reflect the character of the organ. A historic organ should not have to hide behind a modern console. Nor should a misplaced sense of appropriateness insert eighteenth-century keyboards into a Georgian organ which has been radically altered by a major Victorian rebuild. The general appearance of the original console should be recovered, while respecting the effects of later usage, although the usual accretion of tuners' labels, hymn sheets, inappropriate modern electric lights, sockets and switches can be discarded. Pinholes should be filled, and damage to the finish repaired, but the console should not be left looking new.

Old stop labels should not be replaced. If too worn to read, the engraving can be re-filled with black wax or re-engraved, though neither option is perfect. Stop labels which reflect an internal alteration can be left in place. An unattractive stop knob can often signal an inadvisable tonal alteration as well. Do not add department labels or composition pedal labels; it is better to have an explanatory sheet for visiting organists.

Do not replace the bench, for instance with an adjustable bench, unless the new bench can be placed on one side as an option.

The console often retains the original wood finish. It should not be tampered with, but should be used as a model for the exterior of the case.

Wind system

Wind systems tend to be replaced more frequently than any other part of the mechanism, as each generation provides its own answers to the problems of constant supply and even pressure. No eighteenth-century wind system survives in a British church organ, and precious few in chamber organs. The improvements of the first half of the nineteenth century have often been replaced in their turn, and even the bellows systems of the Victorian period have often been replaced by systems adapted to the latest mechanical means of wind supply.

An imperfect wind supply is not compatible with regular performance but we are learning that there is a balance between the mechanical and the musical attributes of a wind system. If a historic wind system seems inadequate, it may be that modern organists are placing greater demands on the wind supply than are strictly necessary and their playing techniques should be adapted to respond. Almost all the historic wind systems surviving in use today will be adequate to today's needs and at their best they are as near perfect as we could hope for.

Most repair work on a wind system has to do with leakage, and the consequent loss of pressure. The original or existing leather should be retained and patched for as long as possible. In ideal circumstances, bellows leather will continue to hold its wind and act as an efficient hinge for two centuries or more, but there is no doubt that frequent use and a dry environment shorten its life. If the whole organ is being dismantled for other reasons, an assessment has to be made about the future life of the leather, for the organ often has to be dismantled to extract the bellows. It is better to replace it than to have the whole organ dismantled again in twenty-five years' time. When re-leathering a bellows, the material, hinging system and the order of leathering the parts should all be noted and reproduced.

The most fugitive but most omnipresent feature in any voicing system is the wind pressure. Just by removing or adding weights the pressure is changed, though it is often recorded on the chest or the tuning pipe. The restorer should record carefully any possible changes in the wind pressure, noting the pressure before the organ is dismantled, looking for clues to previous changes, and assessing the effect of repairs after restoration. There should be no cosmetic alterations to the surface: no whiting of leather, no painting of wood. Neither should the feeders and their pumping handles be removed, even if they are not going to be used. Their presence is part of the historic organ. Our generation is becoming increasingly appreciative of manually operated wind supply systems.

Electric blowers are both a boon and a curse. In an age when cheap manual assistance cannot be obtained, they are an essential but imperfect solution, particularly in organs which were designed with a manual supply. They can be noisy, introduce wind noise into the trunk, and can upset what was originally an excellent wind system with shock waves and slight vibrations. One day, mechanical means for operating manual systems may make electric blowers obsolete.

Blowers have one advantage for the restorer. The constant supply of wind can overcome defects in the wind supply, and reduce the amount that the old reservoir has to move, prolonging its life. Blowers should be introduced tactfully, not by cutting large holes in the side of a historic case. Preferably they should be out of sight, and the trunk and cut-off valve introduced where least noticeable. The wind can enter the old bellows system through the feeder or into the trunk band of the reservoir, or into the trunk from the reservoir to the chest. If there are feeders and pumping handles, there should be a cut-off to prevent the wind escaping through the blower.

Previous systems of raising the wind mechanically should be retained if the space they occupy is not required. It is unlikely that they will be revived, particularly as the power sources are often no longer available, but it would be a pity if their contribution to organ history completely disappeared.

Barrel organs

Barrel organs bring their own problems of repair and restoration. Those driven by clockwork require a knowledge of clockwork as well as organ building, disciplines which rarely go together. The first problem is that their wind supply is usually related to their

fig. 20 Securing the position of loose or deformed barrel pins and staples (the tape indicates the working area, moving from one end of the barrel to the other).

barrel mechanisms, so that the wind retention of the bellows and chest is critical. Since the feeder and reservoir are usually confined to a small space, it is essential that there is no loss of wind, which usually means that the bellows have to be re-leathered, and leaks eliminated from the trunk and chest.

The second problem is that prolonged use has usually upset the pinning of the barrels. Replacing pins which are out of alignment can be more difficult than pinning a new barrel, for the tune has to be reconstructed by stabilizing the pins. It is a painstaking business, and cannot be done cheaply.

Conclusion

There are no simple formulae for the restoration and repair of historic organs, each case throwing up its own dilemmas. It must always be remembered that most restoration work consists of undoing previous restorations. Since conservators are never perfect, they should leave an account of the current work to inform the next generation to tackle the instrument.

appendix 1
Grants

There are several trust funds that sometimes support work on historic organs. The following list gives not only the main sources, but also some of those which only occasionally help, or only in a particular part of the country.

A helpful leaflet, *Grants for Funding Work on Historic Pipe Organs: A Guide*, is available from the Secretary of the British Institute of Organ Studies, Lime Tree Cottage, 39 Church Street, Haslingfield, Cambridge CB3 7JE, at a cost of £2.00. It is available on the web at www.bios.org.uk. Another general leaflet on sources of grant aid and also on methods of fundraising is available from the Council for the Care of Churches. Most public libraries will hold directories of trust funds, and the larger ones have other databases available on CD-ROMs (*Fund Finder*, *Charity Browser*, etc.). The following are helpful for devising a short list and in giving advice on applications:

Directory of Grant-Making Trusts, two volumes, indexed (Charities Aid Foundation, Kings Hill, West Malling, Kent ME19 4TA, Tel: 01732 520 000, and 114–118 Southampton Row, London WC1B 5AA, Tel: 020 7400 2300);

A Guide to the Major Trusts and *A Guide to Minor Trusts* (the Directory of Social Change, 24 Stephenson Way, London NW1 2DP, Tel: 020 7209 5151).

Sources of advice and funding

Funds for major heritage projects in England are made available through the joint grant scheme for churches and other places of worship, administered by English Heritage and the Heritage Lottery Fund. The guidance and technical notes can be obtained from The Heritage Lottery Fund, 7 Holbein Place, London SW1W 8NR (Tel: 020 7591 6000) or English Heritage, 23 Savile appendix 1

Row, London W1X 1AB (Tel: 020 7973 3434). The joint scheme in its current form will last no longer than 2001/2.

Funds for historic instruments in Anglican churches are made available by the Pilgrim Trust and the Esmée Fairbairn Charitable Trust, and administered by the Council for the Care of Churches, Church House, Great Smith Street, London SW1P 3NZ (Tel: 020 7898 1866; Fax: 020 7898 1881; email: enquiries@ccc.c-of-e.org.uk).

The heritage organizations responsible for the various parts of the UK occasionally give funds for the restoration of historic organ cases:

English Heritage, 23 Savile Row, London W1X 1AB (Tel: 020 7973 3434);

CADW, Brunel House, 2 Fitzalan Road, Cardiff CF2 1UY (Tel: 029 2050 0020);

Department of the Environment, Northern Ireland, Environment Service – Historic Monuments and Buildings, 5–33 Hill Street, Belfast BT1 2LA (Tel: 028 90 254754);

Historic Scotland, Longmore House, Salisbury Place, Edinburgh EH9 1SH (Tel: 0131 668 8600).

Projects that can show benefit for the wider community and that may involve the provision of a new instrument rather than the conservation of a historic one could apply to the various Arts Councils, whose funds are now disbursed through the Regional Arts Boards:

The Arts Council Lottery Fund, 14 Great Peter Street, London SW1P 3NQ (Tel: 020 7312 0123; Fax: 020 7973 6571);

The Scottish Arts Council, Edinburgh (Tel: 0131 226 6051);

The Arts Council of Wales, Cardiff (Tel: 029 2037 6500);

The Arts Council of Northern Ireland, Belfast (Tel: 028 90 385200);

Eastern Arts Board, Cambridge (Tel: 01223 215 355);

East Midlands Arts Board, Loughborough (Tel: 01509 218 292) ;

London Arts Board, Covent Garden (Tel: 020 7584 1841);

Northern Arts Board, Newcastle upon Tyne (Tel: 0191 281 6334);

North West Arts Board, Manchester (Tel: 0161 228 3062);
Southern Arts Board, Winchester (Tel: 01962 855 099);
South East Arts Board, Tunbridge Wells (Tel: 01892 515 210);
South West Arts Board (Tel: 01392 218 188);
West Midlands Arts Board, Birmingham (Tel: 0121 631 3121);
Yorkshire and Humberside Arts Board, Dewsbury (Tel: 01924 455 555).

Other sources of funding

The following trusts show regular interest in the organ; there is a long list of others that show occasional interest.

The Diapason Trust, PO Box 5295, Leicester LE2 9ZN;

Foundation for Sport and the Arts, PO Box 20, Liverpool L13 1HB (Tel: 0151 259 5505; Fax: 0151 230 0664);

The Leche Trust, 84 Cicada Road, London SW18 2NZ (for eighteenth-century work only);

The ON Organ Fund, 60 Wellington Road, Pinner, Middlesex HA5 4NH;

The Ouseley Trust, 74 Sweet Briar, Welwyn Garden City, Herts AL7 3EA;

The Secretary, The Pilgrim Trust, Cowley House, 9 Little College Street, London SW1P 3XS (for organs in secular buildings).

appendix 2
Advice

Church of England: Each diocese has at least one Diocesan Organ Adviser who may be contacted through the secretary of the Diocesan Advisory Committee (DAC). The names of DAC secretaries are published in the *Church of England Yearbook*. Requests for advice can also be addressed to the Council for the Care of Churches, Church House, Great Smith Street, London SW1P 3NZ (Tel: 020 7898 1866; Fax: 020 7898 1881; email: enquiries@ccc.c-of-e.org.uk).

The Church in Wales: Each diocese has at least one Diocesan Organ Adviser who may be contacted through the secretary of the Diocesan Advisory Committee (DAC). In the first instance address enquiries to Church in Wales, Cathedrals and Churches Commission, 39 Cathedral Road, Cardiff, CF1 9XF (Tel: 029 2023 1638; Fax: 029 2038 7835).

The Church of Scotland: Robert Lightband, 8 Bingham Terrace, Dundee DD4 7HH.

Roman Catholic Church in England and Wales: The Secretary, Society of St Gregory, The Cottage, 2 Bury's Bank, Greenham Common North, Newbury, Berkshire RG19 8BZ.

Methodist Church: Philip Carter, 50 Bayham Road, Bristol BS4 2DR.

United Reformed Church: The Secretary, URC Musicians' Guild, 'Rainbow's End', 105 Humber Doucy Lane, Ipswich IP4 3NU.

Association of Independent Organ Advisers (AIOA): The AIOA maintains a list of accredited independent organ advisers, available from: The Administrator, The Association of Independent Organ Advisers, Lime Tree Cottage, 39 Church Street, Haslingfield, Cambridge CB3 7JE (Tel: and Fax: 01223 872 190; email: admin@aioa.org.uk; www.aioa.org.uk).

Advice

British Institute of Organ Studies (BIOS): Contact: The Secretary, British Institute of Organ Studies, Lime Tree Cottage, 39 Church Street, Haslingfield, Cambridge CB3 7JE (Tel: and Fax: 01223 872 190; www.bios.org.uk). A brochure on the care of pipe organs, *Sound Advice*, is available from the Secretary.

Institute of British Organ Building (IBO): The IBO maintains a list of organ builders accredited by the IBO after inspection of selected examples of their work. Contact: Administrator, The Institute of British Organ Building, 63 Colebrook Row, Islington, London N1 8AB (Tel: 020 7689 4650; email: administrator@ibo.co.uk; www.ibo.co.uk).

appendix 3
Bibliography

Barclay, Robert, ed.	*The Care of Historic Musical Instruments*, Canadian Conservation Institute, 1997
Berrow, Jim, ed.	*Towards the Conservation and Restoration of Historic Organs*, Church House Publishing, 2000
Bordass, William and Bemrose, Colin	*Heating Your Church*, Church House Publishing, 1996
Burman, Peter, ed.	*Treasures on Earth: A Good Housekeeping Guide to Churches and Their Contents*, Donhead Publishing, 1994
O'Brien, Grant	'Attitudes to musical instrument conservation and restoration', *BIOS Journal*, vol. 6, 1982
Paine, Stephen	*Bats in Churches*, English Heritage, 1998
Plenderleith, Harold and Werner, Alfred	*The Conservation of Antiquities and Works of Art*, Oxford University Press, 2nd edition, 1971
Plowden, Anna and Halahan, Frances	*Looking after Antiques*, Pan Books, 1987
Sandwith, Hermione and Stainton, Sheila	*National Trust Manual of Housekeeping*, Viking/National Trust, 1991
VAT leaflets on organs:	Leaflet 708/1/90, *Protected Buildings (Listed Buildings and Scheduled Monuments)*, available from Customs and Excise offices
	Guidelines for VAT on Church Organs, published by Customs and Excise, dated 27 September 1997.

appendix 4
Research into historic organs

Before embarking on a restoration project of any size, it is essential to authenticate the surviving parts and to find out the important dates and builders associated with the organ. Authenticating and attributing the parts in the organ by examination alone are jobs for an expert. Anybody, with a little persistence, can discover a great deal through written sources, both secondary and primary. The following list gives the likeliest sources for the history of a particular organ. Additional information can often be found in local newspapers, parish magazines, council minutes and churchwardens' accounts, either at the church, in the local library, or in the County Record Offices. The Council for the Care of Churches or the Association of Independent Organ Advisers can offer advice on researchers able to carry out an archaeological survey and inventory of the organ.

The National Pipe Organ Register

Contact www.bios.org.uk/npor.

The British Organ Archive

Contact: The Archivist, The British Organ Archive, Birmingham City Archives, Central Library, Birmingham B3 3HQ, open 09:00 to 17:00, closed Wednesdays and Sundays (Tel: 0121 235 4217).

Nineteenth-century stoplist collections

Henry Leffler's MS collection in Charles Pearce, *Notes on Old London City Churches, Their Organs, Organists, and Musical Associations*, London, 1908

Alexander Buckingham's Notebooks (1823–1842) in Leslie Barnard, 'Buckingham's Travels', *The Organ*, nos. 205–213, July 1972–July 1975

John Sperling's Notebooks (ca 1845–54), ed. in James Boeringer, *Organa Britannica*, London and Toronto, 1989. The additional material supplied by the editor is often unreliable.

Edward Hopkins and Edward Rimbault, *The Organ, Its History and Construction*, Robert Cocks and Company, 1st edition 1855, 2nd edition 1870, 3rd edition 1877. Contains a list of specifications, which was usually brought up to date with each edition.

Selected gazetteers and local studies

Robert Pacey and Michael Popkin, *The Organs of Oxford*, Positif Press, 2nd edition 1997

Nicholas Thistlethwaite, *The Organs of Cambridge*, Positif Press, 1983

Nicholas Plumley, *The Organs of the City of London*, Positif Press, 1996

Rodney Tomkins, *Organs of Derbyshire*, Scarthin Books, 1999

Periodicals

The Organ (quarterly)

The Journal of the British Institute of Organ Studies (annual)

Organ Building (annual)

Organists' Review (quarterly)

Index

NOTE: Page numbers in *italic figures* refer to illustrations.
Churches are indexed under the place where they are located.

access to the organ 33, 44
acoustics 59–60
actions 44, 80–82
adhesives 44, 45, 50–51, 70, 78
advisers 2, 17–18, 22, 90–91
ageing 28, 46
AIOA *see* Association of Independent Organ Advisers
Allan, Sir Hugh 9
alloys
    pipe metal 51–2
alterations 10–13, 20–21, 23, 28, 29
    to action 80–81
    to pipes 53
    tonal 1, 11, 13, 28, 71–2
    see also voice of organ; restoring alterations
appearance of organ 2, 28, 39
Arts Council funding 3, 16, 88–9
Arts Council Lottery Fund 3, 16, 88
Association of Independent Organ Advisers (AIOA) 17, 22, 90, 93
atmospheric stability 34, 37
authenticity 28, 61

bar frame 78
barrel organs 7, 85–6
barrel pins *85*
bats 37
bellows 83, 84
    developments in wind systems 45
    leather deterioration 45–6
BIOS *see* British Institute of Organ Studies
blowers 84–5
bone 49
brass 50, 55
brief for restoration project 23, 24
Brightling church, Sussex 7
British Institute of Organ Studies (BIOS) 17–18, 22, 81, 87, 91
British Organ Archive 18, 93
budget control 26–7
builders *see* organ builders
Burley-on-the-Hill, Rutland *8*

CADW (Welsh Heritage) 88
care of the organ 20, 29, 31, 32–40
cases 2, 15, 32, 39
    care and conservation 56
    surface finishes 55–6
CCC *see* Council for the Care of Churches

Central Council for the Care of Churches 1–3, 22
central heating 35
character of organ 20
    conservation 28, 29, 30
    console 82-3
    stoplists 60–61
choral singing 7, 9
church cleaning 58–9
Church of England, advisers 1, 17–18, 84
church fabric, quinquennial inspection 39
church furnishings
    changing priorities 7, *8*, 9
    effect on acoustics 59
church organists *see* organists
church renovations 58–9
Church of Scotland, adviser 90
Church in Wales, adviser 90
ciphers 40, 75–8, *76*
cleaning 34, 37, 68
cleaning of building 52–3
clockwork driven barrel organs 85-6
cloth 46
condensation 34, 38, 52, 54, 66
cone-tuning 37, 62, 64
conservation
    definition 28
    funding 2–3
    principles 28–31, 41
    and restoration 20–21, 43
console 39, 82–3
consultants 22, 23
    see also advisers
contracts 26–7
corrosion 28, 34, 44, 54–5
    pallet springs *54*, 79
    pipe metal 52–3, 66
    tuning slides 63
costs 14, 19, 23–4, 26–7
Council for the Care of Churches (CCC) 1–3, 16–19, 28, 88, 93
cover for organ 35–7

DAC *see* Diocesan Advisory Committee
damage assessment 43
dampness
    control and prevention 28, 32, 34–5, 54
    deterioration of materials *35*, 44, 49, 70
    situation of organ 12, 34
definitions 29–31
dehydration 32, 35, 38, 40
deterioration of materials 40, 44–51

Index

Diapason Trust 89
Diocesan Advisory Committee 17, 22, 26
Diocesan Chancellor 26
Diocesan Organ Advisers 17, 19, 22, 26, 90
dirt 35–7, 39, 52–3, 70
    affecting reeds 72
DOAs *see* Diocesan Organ Advisers
documenting work 28, 32, 58
draughts 38
dry atmosphere 28, 44, 70
dust 35–7, 38, 58–9
    affecting reeds 72

economic pressures 2, 3
Edgeware, Middx., St Lawrence Whitchurch 10
efflorescence of impurities 67
EH *see* English Heritage
electric actions 81
electric blowers 45, 84
electrolytic corrosion 34, 53, 54
electronic simulation 1, 10
electronic tuning machines 64
English Heritage 3, 15, 16, 87, 88
environmental conditions
    inspection 40
    research before restoration 28
    stability 32, 33–4
environmental damage 12, 13, 20
    case surface finishes 55–6
    deterioration of materials 44–51
    pipe metal 52
equal temperament 62
Esmée Fairbairn Charitable Trust 88
estimates
    builder's estimates 23, 24
    project planning 14, 19
extension 1, 11

fabric
    quinquennial inspection 39
faculty application 22, 26
felt 46
fixed price 26
flue pipes 37
Foundation for Sport and the Arts 89
funding *see* grants
fundraising 23–4
fungi 34, 49

galleries 7, 12, 59–60
gilding 52, 56
glossary of terms 29–30
glues 44, 45, 50–51, 70, 78
grants 2–3, 15–19, 81–3
    application process 16, 19, 23–4
    criteria for grant aid 18
guarantees 27

heat 34, 50
heating 12, 32, 35, 38, 54

Heritage Lottery Fund (HLF) 3, 15, 87
heritage organizations 88
Historic Organs Certificates 18
Historic Scotland 82
history of organs 6–10
    research 87–8
HLF *see* Heritage Lottery Fund
hot air heating systems 38
humidification systems 38
humidity 34–5, 44, 50
    fluctuations 35, 37, 46, 70, 75
    measurement before restoration 35, 58
hygrometers 35
hymn-singing 9

IBO *see* Institute of British Organ Building
insects 37, 38
inspection checklist 39–40
Institute of British Organ Building 17, 19, 81, 91
insurance 33
International Institute of Conservation 28
inventories 22, 23, 52
Ireland, heritage funding 88
ivory 35, 49, 79

Joint Grant Scheme for Churches and Other Places of Worship 16
joints failure 34

key action 9, 39
key depth changes 32
keyboard 35, 79–81

leather 32, 37
    bellows 45–6, 78
    bushes in roller arms 81
    pallets 70, 74, 78
    pneumatic actions 81
    stoppers 70
Leche Trust 89
light 34
lighting 32
liturgy
    changing liturgical fashions 7, 9, 21
    and suitability of organ 5, 6
lottery *see* National Lottery
Lottery Fund *see* Arts Council Lottery Fund
lubrication 70, 76

maintenance 20, 29, 31, 32–40
Manifold Trust 16
matching funding 24
    see also partnership funding
melting points of metals 51
metal 50
    efflorescence of impurities 67
    exterior fittings 55
    flue pipes 37
    parts and fittings 53–5
    pipes 51–3
Methodist Church, adviser 90

Index

mice 32, 36, 37, 46
minimum intervention 43
moths 47
mould 34, 46, 49, 50

National Lottery 3, 15–16
National Pipe Organ Register 18, 93
National Trust 15
new organs 2
Nottingham, St Mary's 11–12
NPOR *see* National Pipe Organ Register

ON Organ Fund 89
The Organ 1
organ builders 23, 24, 26
    choice of 19, 25
    contracts 26–7
    maintenance visits 32
    record of work 28
organ building
    decline 9
    guiding principals 2
    orthodoxy 10
    practice 41–3
    see also reconstruction
Organ Reform Movement 9
organists 5, 9, 21
organs
    assessing importance 18
    decline in popularity 2
    ownership and distribution 7, 9
Organs Advisory Committee 1–3, 22
Organs Committee 1–3, 16–19
Ouseley Trust 89
oxide layer on metal 52, 54

paintwork damage 55–6
pallet springs
    corrosion *61*, 79
pallets 45, 72, 74, 75–9
partnership funding 16
    see also matching funding
parts
    inventory 22, 58
    repair 28
    replacement 11, 34, 43
    retention 28, 41, 43, 54–5
patina 55, 65
payment 27
pedal keys 80
pedalboard 39, 80
permission for projects 26
Pilgrim Trust 16, 88, 89
pinch-tuning 63
pipe foot collapse 65
pipe tops 62–4
pipes 39
    alteration 53
    collapse 53
    conservation 60–61
    corrosion 52–3, 57, 66
    deterioration 51–3, 68

flue 37
patina 59
pitch 61–2
replacement 52, 53
restoration 65–71
storage and transport 64
tuning 61–4
wooden 69–71
pitch 38, 61–2, 63, 65
playing condition 2, 20, 30, 39, 79
playing techniques
    improvisation 9
    wind supply 83–4
pneumatic actions 39, 81
polishes 55–6
pollutants 34
position of organ 7, 11–12, 59–60
price
    contracts 26–7
principal chorus 2, 9
protection of organ 35–7, 58–9
psalmody 7
pulldowns 79
purchase of organs 14, 16

quinquennial inspection 39
quotations 24

rainwater 32
rebuilding 9, 10–13, *12*
    definition 29
    inappropriate *35*
    see also alterations, reconstruction
reconstruction 30
    guiding principles 1
record-keeping 28, 32, 58
Redundant Organ Rehousing Company Ltd 18
reeds 38, 72–4
references, requested from organ builders 25
relative humidity *see* humidity
renovation 29, 41–2, 43
repair 28, 29–30
repair of building 52–53
repair record 32
replacement
    parts 11, 34, 43, 54
    pipe metal 52
research 93–4
restoration 29, 30–31, 41
    arguments for 13, 20–21
    and conservation 20–21, 43
    project management 22–7
    research 93–4
restoration record 28, 32, 58
restoring alterations
    to metal pipes 71–2
    to reeds 73–4
    to wooden pipes 71
retention of parts 28, 41, 43, 60–61
reversibility 28, 29
    adhesives 50, 70

Index

reversing alterations *see* restoring alterations
RH *see* humidity
Roman Catholic Church in England and Wales, adviser 90
roof protection for organ 35–7
runnings 32, 40, 75–8, 76–7

security 33
shrinkage 35, 38, 69, 77
silk backing 34
situation of organ 7, 11–12, 59–60
size 1, 10, 60–61
slider chests 75–9
Society of St Gregory 90
soldering metal pipes 51
sound of organ 28, 31, 59
    indications of damage 32
    see also alterations, tonal
specification 39
spotted metal 52
statutory bodies 15
stop action 81
stop movement 32
stoplists 10, 60–61, 93–4
sub-contractors 27
survey 23, 58
swell 21

temperature 34
    and tuning 37, 38
tinkering 9, 13, 41
tonal alterations *see* alterations, tonal
trust funds *see* grant-giving bodies
tuners 25
tuning 37–8, 39, 44, 61–4
    affected by heating system 38
    electronic 64
    frequency 37, 38, 64
    methods 37, 62–3
    and pipe deterioration 53
tuning slides 37, 62, 63
tuning system 21, 62

undoing restoration 28
United Reformed Church, Musicians' Guild 90

Value Added Tax 24–5
value of organs 20
varnish damage 34, 55
VAT *see* Value Added Tax
ventilation 54
Victorian organs 9, 10, 13, 81
    pitch 61
    restoration/preservation 21
    and spotted metal 52
voice of organ 28, 31, 59
    sounds indicating damage 32
    see also alterations, tonal
voicing 69, 71–2, 73, 74, 84

wear and tear 43, 44
weather-proofing 32
wet rot 34
wind check 40
wind leakage 32, 45, 69–73, 74, 84
wind pressure 45, 68, 84
wind system 45, 83–5
windchests 74–9
wood 47–9
    bleaching 34, 49, 55
    seasoning 48
    shrinkage 35, 38, 69, 77
    stripping of paint and polish 55–6
wooden pipes *see* pipes, wooden
woodworm 32, 37, 49, 50
wool fibres 38